The Wild Excellence

Acclaim for *The Wild Excellence*

Narrating from the borderlands of Yellowstone National Park, Leslie Patten brings us vivid accounts of wolves, grizzlies, the seasonality of ecosystems and tales of prehistoric Indians--all written with a naturalist's eye and woven in a personal network of modern day homesteading, dogs and community. There are times when the best reporting on national parks comes from voices just beyond the legal boundary, close enough for a passionate attachment to the beauty of the land but sufficiently distant for critical appraisal of governmental management.
Leslie Patten is one of those voices.

— Doug Peacock, Author of *Grizzly Years, In the Shadow of the Sabertooth* and other books, Peacock writes and lectures frequently on Western wildlife and climate change. He lives in the northern shadow of Yellowstone Park.

"The Wild Excellence" belongs in every library and personal book shelf. Leslie lets us enter her world of wilderness and all its beauty and wonder. Then encourages us to preserve all that is wild for future generations. Her words, "The grizzly bear's gift to man is the Power of the Present Moment" sums up the essence of this book.

— Dan and Cindy Hartman, *Wildlife Along The Rockies*

Leslie Patten's gripping account of her deep journey into wilderness is funny, hopeful, and profound. At a time when humanity is starting to reap a bitter harvest from its abuse of the environment, she shows us how to have richer and more sustainable lives through our own relationship with the "wild excellence," wherever we find it.
A wonderful book.

— RICK HANSON, PH.D, Author of *Buddha's Brain: The Practical Neuroscience of Happiness, Love, and Wisdom*

"Patten is remarkably careful about describing the research while also imbuing that science with an honest sense of the complexity in such a system, as well as a personal dimension."

— ARTHUR MIDDLETON PhD, Coordinator Absaroka Elk Ecology Project

Leslie Patten combines equal parts passion, reason, adventure, and personal insight to create a glimpse into the spectacular natural treasure she has chosen as her home. She picks her way through both the challenges and opportunities we all face in conserving and managing the wonders of Greater Yellowstone with a keen mind, a full heart, and a delightful flair for storytelling

— CHARLES R. PRESTON, PhD, Senior and Founding Curator, Draper Natural History Museum at the Buffalo Bill Center of the West.

THE WILD EXCELLENCE

Notes from Untamed America

Leslie Patten

ISBN-13: 978-0-9830275-4-6

Published by WordsWorth
2302 Sheridan Avenue
Cody, Wyoming 82414

Book design by R.C. Tafoya
Edited by Lorna Owen
Photograph on page 243 by Michael Patten.
All other photography by Leslie Patten.

Without doubt I praise the wild excellence

Pablo Neruda

CONTENTS

Introduction   xi

Chapter 1 *A Dog and a Lesson*   17

Chapter 2 *First Days*   29

Chapter 3 *The People Before*   55

Chapter 4 *Close Encounters of the Wolf Kind*   85

Chapter 5 *A Most Magnificent Animal*   119

Chapter 6 *Woods, Water, and Wildlife*   139

Chapter 7 *Bear Dreamer*   163

Chapter 8 *Sagebrush Stories*   191

Chapter 9 *Medicine Dog*   215

Chapter 10 *Sacred Land Ethic*   233

Epilogue   245

Acknowledgements   247

Notes   249

Additional Reading   252

You are what your deep driving desire is. As your deep driving desire is, so is your will. As your will is, so is your deed. As your deed is, so is your destiny.

Maitri Upanishads

INTRODUCTION

I walked through the little woods near my cabin to retrieve my trail camera, a nifty little device that snaps photos automatically — one every second when it detects·the heat and movement of an animal. I keep the camouflaged unit stationed along a trail by the springs so I can track all that ventures bye. The camera, a little bigger than my hand, is fixed around a tree with a bicycle cable and a heavy lock. I opened the front, scrolled through the menu to see if I had any photos. Twenty three.

I glanced over the Douglas fir and Englemann spruce trees that make up these little woods. Their sweet spring sap was flowing and the scent wafted on a slight breeze. In just a month, the forest will come alive, green and thick. But in today's mid-May chill, the shrubs were still leafless, so any movement would quickly catch my eye. A few patches of late snow remained. I looked around for clues of who'd been visiting but saw only several deer tracks in the wet snow. *Mostly deer on these photos I bet.*

I walked back to the cabin, a few hundred yards through forest and field, and placed the memory chip in my computer. One by one the photos loaded in, revealing all the visitors in the last few days. A boar grizzly bear. A beautiful mother black bear with two cubs of the year. A young female cougar. Two wolves traveling through to a den on the other side of the river. A yearling moose. A small red fox and of course, deer.

Apart from a sprinkling of human residents, these are my neighbors, along with a host of other wildlife visitors. In a real sense, they are the inhabitants of these lands and I am the temporary visitor, at best a caretaker of their home. My own house sits within the map of what's now called The Greater Yellowstone Ecosystem, an area of over 27 million acres, spanning three states, five National Forests, the National Elk Refuge, Grand Teton National Park and the centerpiece: Yellowstone National Park. This enormous region of protected public and private lands is necessary to sustain the large animals now so rare in the lower 48. The Greater Yellowstone Ecosystem is one of the last and largest mostly intact ecosystems in the temperate world.

I first came to Wyoming in 1972. I was a teenager on a road trip with friends. We stopped in Jackson, loaded our backpacks with supplies, and spent three weeks hiking the backcountry of the nearby Tetons and Wind River ranges. I was sixteen and vowed to return someday. A stream in a forest forges new channels over time, yet ultimately works its way to the river. Twenty five years later, I honored that promise and found my way back to Wyoming. I had fallen in love long ago and never forgot.

A raw, elemental place, Wyoming drew me in a different way. It seemed to hold the essence of what was required to be a human being: A silence of space that clears the mind of senseless chatter. A landscape demanding vigilance and clear-eyed thinking — a brilliant warm day turns into a fierce snowstorm; the crackling of dry leaves and a grizzly appears. Its solitude and vast distances awakened my vulnerability and kindness — I may not care for my neighbors' politics or drinking problem, but he'll sure as hell be there for me when I'm broke down on the road or lost in the mountains. Here there was no hiding from the existential quandary of our aloneness. The sharp edge of this kind of living made sense and just seemed real. In my forties, I began returning summers to backpack with no intention of moving here full-time from California. Yet over time things worked out differently. This place, Wyoming, and more precisely, the Absaroka-Beartooth mountains, are my psychic center and now my permanent residence.

Living day to day, season by season, in the wildlife corridors next to Yellowstone National Park, I've had the opportunity to view the changes in the landscape, the migratory patterns of the animals and explore as many nooks and crannies as I could possibly day hike to. As Henry David Thoreau once said, twenty square miles is more than enough for one man to explore in a lifetime. I've got much more than that in just my backyard.

These lands that millions of people visit every year are the closest we still have to what Lewis and Clark saw in their journey west. Mostly we see shadows of the past — bits of large herds that once roamed here; tipi rings, petroglyphs, or arrowheads of the nomadic peoples who called these lands their homes; compressed areas of wilderness once so vast as to be incomprehensible. But we can fill in through our imagination, and use those faculties to envision, restore, and solve the deep and pressing problems of wild lands and wildlife we face in the 21st century.

And of course, not only wildlife benefits through our efforts. We need these places to restore our spirit. City parks and open spaces are calming and invigorating, but deep refreshment can only come through large tracts of lands free of mechanical and technological implements — places where roaming and wandering for days can happen; where the natural order of things is set right and free; where entire ecosystems are whole.

Through the telling of my tales, my journey back to a place that moved me in my youth, a place never forgotten that lives in each and every one of us, I hope to bring alive this conversation in public and private of how special these places are, how important they are to preserve, and to inspire new and creative approaches to solve the complex issues of space and the room to roam in our ever-increasingly complicated world.

"By not knowing, not hoping to know, and not acting like we know what's happening, we begin to access our inner strength."

Pema Chodron

CHAPTER 1

A Dog and a Lesson

It was August, the day was cool and threatening rain, but I decided to hike the trail down to the Clark's Fork River of the Yellowstone and take Soona, my eleven year old Golden Retriever. In spite of her age just the day before she'd hiked eight miles without any trouble. Tom, the seller of the cabin I had just bought, told me to take a lunch and absolutely do this hike. It was a 'must see'. Unmarked from the road, I made several passes before I found the dirt cutoff leading to the trail. Mostly used by locals, the forest service sign marking the trailhead had been removed. The route follows along flats and meadows high above the river that lies a thousand feet below. This precipitous canyon was formed millions of years ago by water and ancient glacial ice. The hike was four miles each way. In the first three miles, a hiker takes in the broad vistas of plateau and deep canyon, with a backdrop of the rising flanks of the Beartooth Mountains. At the two mile mark, a faint side route leads to a viewpoint of a waterfall. Standing on the cliff's edge, the dizzying drop below reveals the tortuous white water of Wyoming's sole Wild and Scenic river. As the hike progresses, the broad plateau narrows, and you're left hugging multicolored sedimentary massifs. Suddenly, the narrow shelf of a trail ends, and begins a series of crude switchbacks dropping a thousand feet in one mile. Tom also warned me there was no water until you reached the river. So I brought several quarts of water for Soona and a quart of water for myself.

I also planned to bring a portion of my brother Richard's ashes to scatter in the canyon. He had died two years before and I had heard the canyon walls were "a cathedral." We'd hiked the Grand Canyon together when I was younger, and he shared my love of the West and its 'larger than life' landscape. This seemed like a perfect place for my brother. I filled a coffee can with the ashes. Soona and I started the hike. After about one and a half miles I was careful to give water to the dog. But soon she was taking longer and longer rests, reluctant to continue. Her panting increased; I gave her more water. At around the three mile mark, the steep switchbacks down to the river begin, all very exposed with loose rock. You can see

Soona in the Beartooth Mountains

the river from the top of the canyon. Poor Soona was panting very heavily now, yet I needed to push her on. All the water was 1000' below.

Half way down the steep canyon wall, Soona refused to move. I knew my dog was in real trouble and I had to give her my complete attention. I abandoned my plan with my brother's ashes and ceremony. There was a strangeness to the moment: I needed to attend to the living — my dog who was in distress — instead of doing a ceremony for the dead. Plus I needed the coffee can for a dog drinking vessel. I said some quick words, threw Richard's ashes over the side of the switchbacks, and poured all the remaining water I had into the coffee can. Soona drank the whole thing. Now, out of water, Soona, still panting, was lying down, desperately hot. We were still over 750 feet up from the river, hanging on exposed switches. I tied her to a tree, thinking I'd make the descent myself for more water. I started down but then thought the better of it. It would be a long time and a long haul back up to bring her water. She just had to follow me farther down. I untied her, and we started again. Luckily her legs still worked and she started again.

This scenario of stopping and resting for extended stretches repeated itself many times. It seemed like we'd been doing this for over half an hour, and still Soona hadn't had enough water. She was obviously in serious trouble. But now with the river within a quarter mile I left her above and made my way down to the river bank. Once there I filled up the coffee can, all my bottles plus a camelback I'd brought. Running back up the steep hillside to meet her, I let her drink out of the coffee can, refilling it over and over with the bottles. Still she didn't move, so I ran back down to the river, filled up, then hurried back to let her drink some more.

In just a few minutes she'd drank several quarts of water. It was at that moment that I realized she was having a very serious heat stroke. Finally, after much prodding, she made it to just a few hundred feet from the river. I knew she'd never make the return trip home, and that if I wanted my dog to survive, I needed somehow to get her into the water. Her back legs, however, had given out completely. She no longer had any strength in them, and I wasn't sure if she was loosing motor control of them entirely. She was just scooting along and didn't even want to scoot. Soona weighed over eighty pounds, and although I could not carry her, I was dragging her along to the water's edge – my Soona who loved the water.

By and by I got her to the river — the Clark's Fork of the Yellowstone River, not a little stream. Much of the summer it can be a rushing current. By mid-August, the river slows in most places. Fortunately there was a sand bar nearby. I moved her to an eddy where she could drink as much as she wanted, when she wanted, and keep her tummy cool. Although the day was very humid, it was still overcast. That could work in her favor, I thought

Now I was at a crossroads. Should I stay with her overnight and hope she could make it out in the morning? I had emergency supplies in my daypack. Or should I leave her and hike back for help? I decided there was plenty of daylight left, and that I wasn't sure she'd be much better in the morning. So I unloaded some of the weight from my pack like the coffee can and the bottle and left some of my clothes — my hat, my sandals — thinking Soona would have my scent and understand that I would be returning. What I knew was that I had to return for her before dark. Old and helpless, she'd be someone's meal; on the other hand if she got enough energy and she tried to follow me back up the trail, then for sure I'd lose her for good.

I began the long hike back up the canyon. I hadn't eaten but worse, I had no fresh water, only the river water. This I didn't want to drink for fear of intestinal parasites like Giardia that are in most mountain streams. It was 12:30 when I began the climb. I was anxious about leaving Soona. I worried if I would see her again; how I would retrieve her and who would help me? I had noticed a jeep road on the other side of the creek, but during the several hours I was hiking I hadn't seen a soul, on foot or in an ATV. I'd never been in a place so isolated before. I had been used to the Sierras, or Wyoming's Wind River range, where people come around frequently.

I hoped to make it back to the car by 2:30 p.m. That would give me two hours to hike the four miles, yet I didn't make it to the lookout point until 2:00. From there it was another two miles to the parking area. I was lightheaded, hot headed, thirsty and winded,

By and by I got her to the river

especially climbing up the canyon walls. From hiking so fast, I'd already developed a raw blister on my right heel. I put some moleskin on and kept going. I estimated I'd be at the car by 3:00 or later and that bothered me. That meant fewer hours of daylight in order to do all that was necessary to retrieve Soona. Eventually I saw the road cut. I left the trail and headed for the highway. The highway embankment was incredibly steep. Go slow. Focus I told myself. By the time I reached the road I was shaking.

Chief Joseph Highway is a scenic byway leading to the Park. In the summer, tourists come through on motorcycles and motor vehicles. People don't expect to see hitchhikers flagging them down, or you might say, standing completely in the road to obstruct motorists as I did. A young couple in a small four-seater stopped and opened the door. Their back seats were crammed to the brim with all their luggage and camping gear. I mumbled something and climbed into the front seat, pushing the woman over. "Please, just drop me down the road. I need to call the sheriff to help get my dog who's down in the canyon." I must have looked a sight. That couple had their five minutes of a strange encounter on their tourist trip into Yellowstone.

The fortuitous thing was that I just happened to have the Deputy Sheriff's cell phone number in my car. Sheriff Dan lived up the road about ten minutes from this trailhead. To make ends meet, I'd heard he also did backhoe work as well as horse wrangling. I had planned to call him later about some work on my spring. I dialed the number; he answered and said he'd be right over.

As I waited for him, I tried desperately to calm myself. My head was burning hot, my limbs felt like putty, my legs were trembling. The sheriff appeared and as I began to explain the situation, I started having an asthma attack.

"Are you okay?" Dan asked.

Oh my God, I certainly didn't want this to become a rescue for me. I took some deep breaths and, attempting to take hold of the situation in a practical manner, I asked, "Can we get some horses to retrieve the dog?"

The sheriff knew the canyon well.

"No way a horse can take that dog up. The dog won't go for it and it's too steep for the horse. It'd be dangerous for the horse. Driving here, I contacted the local animal rescue. They don't rescue dogs, only cattle and horses."

Apparently, I thought, dogs aren't worth anything in Wyoming except sentiment.

Dan looked at my Jeep Liberty. "There's an ATV road on the other side of that river. I think your Jeep will make it." I told Dan I didn't know how to get there.

"You have to drive over the mountain pass, down into the desert, and into the town of Clark. Drive through the town, over the county dirt road. That will take you up to the mouth of the Clark's Fork Canyon. From there the road is an old riverbed. It's bad but I think you can make it in your vehicle."

I asked if someone could go with me. I'd heard about that road — more of a wash than a road. It took a skilled individual on an all terrain vehicle to drive it and I wasn't experienced enough in that sort of driving. Plus my mind was racing, my body depleted, and I was over-amped with adrenaline. I just couldn't drive there alone. In addition, fording that river I doubted I'd be able to do it without the support of a rope and another person. Thinking he was the sheriff, I assumed I was pleading with him to help me. Instead he suggested my neighbor across the street who owns a horseback riding summer camp for teenagers. I followed the sheriff's car down the road and over to some outbuildings the ranch owned. All the campers and most of the adults had gone on a pack trip to the Beartooth Mountains. Luckily, one of the daughters was around, along with a ranch hand whom I had met earlier that spring when he helped me change a flat tire.

"I need your help, Josh," I said.

The Sheriff made sure we had some good rope for the wide river crossing; the three of us, Josh, Allie and I, piled into my jeep with Josh driving. Josh and Allie, both around twenty-two years of age, in good Wyoming fashion were quiet most of the trip. I sat in the back and was the chatterbox. Nervous, all I could think about was Soona and how long she'd been lying there, if she was still lying there. It was now close to 4 p.m.

Finally, after more than an hour, we arrived at the town of Clark, nestled at the mouth of the impressive canyon. The steep walls of the gorge towered thousands of feet above us. We began the drive up the ATV road, a riverbed with huge rocks to go around and over. With young Josh driving, we proceeded slowly, bouncing the car this way and that over each boulder. I barely noticed all the scraping sounds the large rocks were making on the car's underneath.

It took over an hour to go four miles. Periodically Allie would ask, "Do you recognize anything?" But I'd come down the other side of the river, from the top of the bench. I'd never been up from the mouth. After four miles, I saw the wall where I thought Soona and I had come down from. And I was correct. Allie spotted Soona; then Josh saw her. From the backseat I could barely see her — yet she was moving, they said. By this time it was 6:30 at night. Soona had been alone for six hours.

We stopped the jeep in a wide area where Josh could turn

around. The river was a few hundred feet away, through willows, cacti, and dense shrubbery, and across two narrow tributaries. As I called to her, Soona looked back up the trail where she and I had come down from. Then the old girl turned to the direction of my voice and saw me across the river. Tired but standing, her tail wagging like a muscle that never knows fatigue, I suppose she always trusted I'd come back for her, so she just waited. And in that moment all the weariness and anxiety drained from my body. I was simply and completely happy to see her again.

Josh, Allie and I crossed the first tributary, our boots filling with water, and then crossed the second one. The river was wide but not flowing too fast. Allie said she'd go; I easily relented. She was tall and strong and I knew she could handle the river better than I could right now. As she started across she told me to command Soona to stay on the other side till she could get to her. We didn't want her jumping in and then swept away in the downstream current. The Clark's Fork is considered an unrunnable river, which would make it impossible to catch her.

Soona appeared recovered enough to be able to stand, a good sign. Allie held the rope while Josh let out the lead. This was Allie's lifeline and security. At the midway point, the water came up to Allie's chest. I was trying to control Soona but I was too far away. Soona couldn't resist jumping in; she started to swim. Thankfully, Allie was able to catch her collar. Soona's back legs were still weak. When she reached me, we put a sweatshirt around her waist, and with that little lift, she was walking. As we got close to the car, the cacti were overwhelming and hard for the dog to avoid in her wobbly condition. Josh picked her up, and unlike her usual self, Soona didn't struggle but just lay limp in his arms.

We got home after 8:00 pm. I was as exhausted as the dog. A vet told me later, "You know, you did just the right thing by dragging her into the water. By keeping her tummy cool, you probably saved her life."

I had owned my cabin for only six months and knew few people in the valley. But within days, it seemed everyone had heard one version or another of the story. They'd listened to it on their scanners, a piece of equipment most people have around these parts. When I'd meet people that summer, invariably they'd ask, "So you're the woman with the dog?" I was learning about life in a small community and life in a true wilderness, fast.

One day I was at the small local store and restaurant a few miles up the road talking with a district ranger who had asked about the incident. He had some advice for me.

"You ought to carry a gun. Not for bears, but in case something like this happens, you're far out on the trail, and you've got to shoot your dog."

Love, not reason, should make decisions. Decisions based on reason, and not love, are karmic. Therefore, let the heart be your intelligence.

Adi Da Samraj

CHAPTER 2

First Days

I'm a California girl, by birth and at heart. When I was little, my father used to ask, "Do you want to go to the snow?" We'd jump into the car, drive up to the San Gabriel mountains outside of Los Angeles, throw snowballs, make a snowman, then drive home by dinnertime to bask in the warm L.A. sunshine. In those early days in Southern California, no one went skiing for the weekend. But now here I was, spending my first winter in Wyoming, a state with so much snow that their highway department teaches other states how to build the best snow fences in the world.

I wasn't totally bereft though. While living in northern California I'd worked for over twenty years as a landscape designer and habitat consultant, developing a sensitivity to weather, seasonal changes, moisture, wind patterns, and how the contours of land affects living things. Concurrently, I assisted with a federal spotted owl study, and volunteered as a naturalist in Muir Woods/ Muir Beach instructing school children. When tracks and tracking began occupying my attention, I joined a tracking club in Marin County, mostly comprised of young people in their late twenties and early thirties. I was thrilled to see a revitalization of interest in nature that I hadn't seen for a long time, especially with the advent of the new techno-generation. We'd meet once a month on a sandy dune in Point Reyes. The dunes made great tracking, but I knew snow was even better. I planned to use it to my advantage this first winter.

I first got the crazy idea of buying a place in Wyoming returning from a backpack in the Wind Rivers. I'd been driving out every summer from the Bay Area since 1997. The backpack adventures started as necessary solace and healing. I was newly divorced from a twenty-plus year marriage, raising my young son mostly on my own. My natural instincts from childhood kicked in — I remembered how restored I always felt from the backpack trips of my youth in the Sierras and mountains of Southern California. That was where I needed to be now — during this time of intense stress and grief.

I usually took Soona, although when I didn't I'd include Yellowstone in the itinerary. Those trips, normally six or seven days in the backcountry, were something I dreamt about all winter, mapping my route, looking forward to that tiny window of time the high country has to offer. July is too full of mosquitoes, September the weather is too unpredictable. I always shot for the second week of August.

Somewhere around the end of my sixth backpack summer in the Winds, I began the interminable drive back to California. I watched the jagged peaks of the Continental Divide disappear in my rear view mirror and wondered why I was returning to the Bay Area. This place was starting to seem like the idea of home I'd always been looking for. It was calling to me more strongly each year.

Michael, my son, was now in high school. He was working

on his learner's permit and the carrot of endless driving practice back and forth from California was an enticement to accompany me on a Winds trip. We planned to hike into Pyramid Lake and over two high mountain passes, dropping down to the eastern side of the Winds. Unfortunately, a freak summer system brought us heavy rain almost every day of our trip. That trip may have been the deciding factor. What if I could have a cabin near the Winds where I could spend a month or more, and watch the weather for the best pack days? I first began looking around Pinedale, the jumping off town to the Wind River Range. But the Pinedale area was rapidly changing with the advent of the Jonas Field, a massive fracking project. As luck would have it, the following year in 2004, I changed directions and went with friends into the Beartooth-Absaroka Range. On my drive home I planned to stop in the Wind Rivers eastern side for a short solo trip. Passing through Cody, I was impressed that this gateway town had a community feeling. I decided to explore finding property in its' vicinity.

My plan all along, if I even really had one, was to spend more money on the land than on the structure. I hoped for a cabin that I could at least live in during the summer months, and either build or remodel. But the land was what I was dreaming about. That winter, in February of 2005, I flew back to Cody and met a realtor. Al showed me not homes or properties, but spent a day acquainting me with the Cody environs. I explained to Al that I wanted a property with a stream, trees, somewhat secluded but not isolated from neighbors.

"What you want comes up every ten years or so," he told me. He had nothing to show me. I told him to keep me in mind.

Over six months later, in late September, I received a call from Al. "There's a property down the South Fork which I think you should see. It's unusual and fell out of escrow, but it will be on the market and sold again within a few days." I hopped on a plane the following day.

Although that property wasn't for me, I asked Al if there was anything else, anywhere, that I should see. I had a few hours left before my flight home. He told me about a property, not on the market, off a nearby scenic byway. The parents who owned it had died and their kids weren't sure they wanted to sell. They'd been discussing it for a year.

"Show it to me anyways, in case they do sell someday."

I had no idea where this area he was talking about was. I'd never been on this road before despite all my time in Wyoming. Al told me the property was about an hour from town. I was nervous about the distance. I had envisioned living far enough away to have some space but much closer to a populated community. An hour, over a mountain pass, seemed very isolated.

As we climbed up to the pass, the scrub of the high desert faded into pines and douglas firs. It was fall and the grasses were a tawny brown. We rounded an impressive large deep-red butte. At the top of the pass, 8800 feet, we stopped for the view. I'd never seen topography such as this before. The entire landscape, west to east, changed radically in one sweep. From south to northwest were the majestic and rugged volcanic Absaroka Mountains, the eastern edge of Yellowstone. Over a thousand feet below lay a wide basin, formed by an ancient glacial lake. In the foreground was a tipped butte that mimicked a steamboat and so bore that name. Framing the valley to the north, a large white mountain made of limestone and marble loomed. Beyond it's craggy white peak, another even higher peak rose tall as if to guard this magnificent valley. As my eye swung left to right towards the north, a perfectly flat mesa sat near the mouth of this basin. The Beartooth Mountain range, some of the oldest rocks on earth discovered there, hung as a backdrop. To the north and east lay an expansive plateau with a deeply cut gorge like a ribbon running through it. And although my knowledge and understanding of geology is sketchy, anyone could see that the complexity of the formations were enough to make a geologist drool, and every man feel awed by the immensity. I was standing in place, yet viewing vast passages of time in a single expanse — from the beginnings of our earth through billions of years of uplifts, erosions, glacial and volcanic episodes, and oceans and tides ebbing and flowing. I would learn later that geologists come from all over the world to study these areas. That there is a prominent peak in Cody, which virtually slid in a matter of minutes via a fault from Cooke City, over forty miles to the Northwest — and that landmark, named Heart Mountain, is upside down! This was mountain building in action, visible almost before my eyes.

As we wound down the summit's steep side, the views became more and more breathtaking. At the bottom we turned onto a dirt road and drove up for several miles.

"Do they plow this in the winter?"

Al thought they did but wasn't sure.

We turned up a narrow driveway. There it was, a funky log cabin built in 1957 by a doctor from the East who came out to enjoy a dude ranch nearby.

When first constructed the house had a large sleeping porch. The previous second owners did a major remodel of splitting the bedroom in two, yet leaving half a window in each room. They added a second bath and an attic. But the walls and ceilings of all these new rooms were left raw. Mice had been coming in through the unfinished ceiling from the attic. Al told me they'd finally gotten the mice under control. I saw d-Con piles in every corner.

The second owners, the sellers, lived in Washington state; it appeared they'd furnished the cabin with used items from their primary home once they were either no longer in style or about to be trashed. The living room and entry had orange shag carpet. The small kitchen contained the original linoleum floor, in pieces. The bedroom and hallway floors consisted of carpet scraps.

Al explained that these cabins came 'as is,' which meant all the furniture and trimmings. I'd purchased a few homes before and this was new to me. I figured that was great. I could discard what I wanted but wouldn't have to — initially at least — purchase anything. Silverware, beds, bedding, towels, pots and pans, everything would stay. Except, Al said, the heads. They wanted to take the elk and deer mounts that were on the walls. Frankly, I was relieved.

The living room, the main area, was about thirty by twenty-five feet and contained so much furniture you could barely move. There were two full size picnic tables with two wooden benches, two sofas — one over nine feet — an easy chair, several 50's style standing lamps, a wooden coffee table, two six foot handmade storage benches, a few storage chests, and lots of books and games. A large picture window set the stage for the living room. It looked east over the Clark's Fork Canyon and an impressive prominence called Bald Ridge.

It was love at first sight. It was the cabin I'd been envisioning. Just as I was imagining myself in this house, Al said, "Do you want to see the upper cabin?"

We drove his large Ford 4WD up a steep and narrow road behind the house. It turned out the main house was actually situated at the front of the six acres, at the bottom of a small rise. Most of the land was above, on a flat that butted up against Forest Service land.

All but two sides of the property were adjacent to Forest Service land.

The second cabin was at the very back of the property, well hidden. It was a one-room log structure, no water, no electricity. An old barrel stove sat directly on the wooden floor. The floor was dark from years of pine pitch dripping from the ceiling, but the cabin was well-built, set on a concrete foundation that someone had recently chinked.

"What's this cabin for?" I asked Al.

"Probably built here as a hunting cabin. The elk pass through here. This is their winter range."

Inside, the cabin was stuffed with unused paneling and other junk, leftovers from the remodelling of the main cabin. The owners had clearly been using it as a big storage shed.

"I want it." I told Al and asked him for comps and a fair price. He gave me a number of comps, and I told him to offer a little more and that would be my only price. I wasn't interested in haggling. I wanted the property, but I was already reaching well beyond what I could afford. I was just going by my heart and the seat of my pants here.

"What's up the county road?" I asked Al.

He told me the dirt road went directly west and ended about five miles from the Yellowstone Park boundary line. Time was running out, I needed to get back to Cody to catch my plane. I'd only been at the cabin for half an hour, didn't know the first thing about this new area, and I had just made an offer. Most people see a home and say "I could live here," but for some reason the first words out of my mouth to Al were, "I could die here." This was the land for me.

* * * * * *

The week I was supposed to close escrow, my sister-in-law died unexpectedly. My brother, her husband, had died just two years earlier. It was a big blow. I delayed the December closing, flew to Washington D.C. to identify her body, then flew into Cody. I was in quite a state. Everything was a bit surreal, but I wanted to spend at least a few days in my cabin instead of completing the sale by mail.

I hoped the county road really was plowed in the winter as Al thought. I rented a Jeep at the airport and drove in. It was cold, around minus 5 degrees. Al accompanied me. He knew that there were some sticky things that I would have no idea how to handle. He must have looked at this lady from the Bay Area and felt sorry for her, knowing I'd need a primer. A summer cabin in the mountains needs to have the pipes drained before winter comes so they don't burst. The cabin had been drained by the owners that fall. We needed to turn the water on in order for me to stay there. A large wooden box with a cover sat by the front door. This box housed a small plumbing nightmare of pipes and gate valves. A pressure pump sat on a narrow shelf inside. Without the pump, only a trickle of water came through.

All my water comes from a spring several hundred yards up on National Forest. From the spring runs an underground pipe to deliver the water. In order to turn the water on for the cabin, I needed a 'key,' similar to the keys that turned on old irrigation systems. But this key was a six foot metal pole. That's because the frost line in Wyoming is six feet down. The idea was to lower the pole key into a three inch PVC upright pipe. At the bottom, six feet below, was a valve. Fiddling around, you could catch the valve onto the key by feel, deliver a quarter turn to the right, and open the valve to the spring. Adjacent to the spring valve was a similar tube six feet down that held a drain valve. This needed to be turned quarter to the left to close it. This was done before opening the spring water. When you left, to drain the cabin, simply close the spring and open the drain. It all seemed simple enough, except after years and years, dirt had piled up around the valve heads, making contact difficult. Over the next few years, I sometimes spent more than one half hour just trying to get the key to catch the valve head. One time I missed my plane struggling with this. But this first time, freezing in the cold, we were, between the two of us, able to make it work.

Opening the spring valve was only the first step. Next I had to get into the belly of the outdoor box. Following the maze of pipes, we determined which valves to close or open to allow the water to run through the pressure pump. Unfortunately, we couldn't get the pump to work. Maybe it had some water in it that had frozen up its parts. No matter, neither of us could figure it out. So now we had to change the valve set-up to run the water directly into the cabin. Al pulled on a ball valve handle to open it. Because it was so cold outside, the handle broke off completely. Luckily it was broken in the open position. This whole set-up was really funky. In my landscaping business we call this a 'homeowner fix' and I vowed to change it as soon as money permitted.

I had water, at least at a trickle. Now I needed heat. The cabin had a wall heater in the hallway by the bedrooms. It was a gas heater, but the house didn't have a gas line. I assumed it was another item brought from Washington. My main source of heat was the wood stove insert. There was lots of wood left luckily, but all of it was spruce. What I didn't know then, but learned over time, is that spruce has a very low BTU output. That meant that I could burn and burn and it would take days for the cabin to heat up. The windows were old wooden sills with single pane glass. Most of them didn't open and all of them leaked like crazy. Somehow, that wood stove was able to heat the main room up to about 50 degrees. I found every blanket in the house and bedded up next to the wood stove on the mouse infested nine foot couch for the next three days.

The days flew by exploring the left-over contents of the cabin — logbooks chock-full of dates of visitors and important improvements like 'today the fire pit was built so we can have outdoor fires' or so-and-so 'brought the two mules,' inventorying the kitchen and bedroom items, exploring the books left, or simply feeling the 'vibes' of the obvious family fun summer vacations the previous owners had there. They'd owned the place for over twenty-five years. Anyone can get a good feeling of a person's life by exploring their home. Since the cabin was almost left exactly 'as is' for me, I could feel all the love and happy moments this family had shared here.

But what of the original owners, the Firors? They'd built this cabin in the late 50's. I knew nothing of them. All traces of their presence were gone, or so I thought. Those first nights alone in the cabin, already broken up by the death of my sister-in-law, I was highly sensitized to invisible dimensions at work on that land. After spending the day going through the stuff of the owners, I laid down to sleep, wondering about the Firors. That night I had a dream with powerful symbols of Christianity: the Pope visiting San Francisco, crosses and rosaries. I myself am not religious nor Christian. The symbolism in the dream was unusual.

A few days after this dream I was scheduled to fly home to California. Few people are in the valley for the winter as most have summer homes. But one of my neighbors, who'd been coming out every summer for over thirty years, just happened to be here for the Christmas holidays. I called them and went over for a short visit. They had known the 'Doc.' I asked them what he was like.

"Oh, he was a special person and a good friend. A very religious person, he even used to like to lead a local sermon in the valley on some Sundays. You know, that upper cabin of yours was his study, where he studied religious texts. He liked to go up there, and be alone, meditate, write and study the bible."

I was floored. I felt like I'd had a visitation from Doc Firor, letting me feel his presence and relationship to my house along with the sellers'.

Finding my home was unusual in itself. I tell people 'it found me.' It was if this unique valley snuck into the tunnels of my psyche, working little miracles, dreams and synchronicities to attract me here.

* * * * * *

"My dad always said 'Keep two of everything in your shop,'" a neighbor who lived in town but kept up his parents' nearby cottage told me. With the nearest store over an hour away, you didn't want to come up a screw short when putting a project together.

I had no 'shop', only an old leaky metal shed with no floor or electricity. The following July I sorted through the leftover tools, nails and miscellaneous items. There was a lot of useful stuff and other items, like jugs of old car oil, that had to be taken to the dump. A winter-killed squirrel had curled up to die in one corner. Forty five miles to the nearest store, a person has to become a jack-of-all-trades. A small annoyance, like a faucet leak, required not only parts, but also a plumber who might charge $300 travel time for a 45-minute job. I just had to learn to become handy and equip this tiny shack-of-a-tool shed. It didn't take long after the purchase to realize living here required a kind of physicality I wasn't used to.

I've always been fairly athletic and liked to work with my hands, but I'd also battled an autoimmune disease for over twenty years that required cautiousness when it came to over-exerting myself. I easily developed soft-tissue sprains and strains, had back, hand and feet problems from the disease. Here I was in the place I'd forever longed to be but hadn't considered nor known the stakes.

Fence work was my initiatory experience with the demands of hard living in this wild place. In that first June, Joe and Patricia, friends from California, used my cabin for a week while I was in the Bay Area.

"If you're surrounded by National Forest," Joe asked, "why don't you just take the fence down?"

Good question I thought. I had a rickety but semi-functional three-strand barbed wire fence. Good metal posts were interspersed with cut tree limbs not pounded into the ground, along with sagging wire that was spliced with extra pieces in so many places it appeared swollen. This marked my property line. Yes, I figured, why not take it down! Lucky for me my impulsive side was dampened by the sheer volume of other projects.

Wyoming is a 'fence-out' state. That means that if you don't want cattle running around your yard, it's your responsibility to fence them out. If a cow is on your property and gets hurt, you are responsible. What's more, if you kill a cow on a highway with your car and that cow is legally on open range, you are responsible for paying market value for that cow, even if you are killed or injured in the accident. Cattle are king in a state where ranching weaved the patterns of progress on this land. Cows and calves can be savvy about getting under or over fences; or tearing them down by rubbing against them. So you can have a fence, but if it's not to state standards and heights, and a cow is on your property, it's your fault. In general, a lawful fence under Wyoming statute is a 3-strand barbed wire fence, but there's also some wiggle room under the law.

Because our national forests still run grazing allotments — allowing livestock to graze public lands at exorbitantly low, essentially subsidized, prices — cattle move through here every summer. It's an outdated custom from over hundred years ago. The Bureau of Land Management and the Forest Service, collectively, lose over $100 million a year with these grazing programs. One of the reasons the Forest Service was initially created was to set up a fair system of grazing. Cattle ranchers moved into the vast ranges of the West after the buffalo and Indians were gone. Without any controls, they grazed the lands as they wished and had major battles over territory.

I border National Forest on two sides. I hadn't seen any cows on the forest lands yet, but once I heard this, I headed to the back end of the property to repair a gate. The previous owners had left some basic fencing material — a simple fencing tool that looked part hammer, part pliers, with a pick-like utensil on one side; some clips and heavy fencing staples. I examined how the fence was constructed. This really didn't appear complicated I thought. I could see how Tom, the previous owner, had used the clips to hold the wire in place around the metal stakes, and when a wooden post came along, the staples were hammered into it. Although a fencing tool is a beautiful utilitarian instrument with many fencing functions I had yet to learn, I could at least see that the 'pick' end could pull the staples out; the 'hammer' end could drive them in; the 'pliers' part could be used to hold and twist the clips around the barbed wire to the metal stake. I was in business. This is not hard!

I decided on replacing a sagging wire that was only a 35' stretch. I'd start small. I wound the wire around a large firm wooden post and used the staples. Then I pulled it along to each metal stake, clipping the wire to the post as I went. When I got to the last large wooden post, I pulled it hard to stretch it, then pounded in a staple to hold it. I stood up to examine my work. The wire wasn't taut — stretched yes but too saggy. I repeated this effort but just could never use my muscle strength to make the wire tight enough. *How in the world do they do it?* I wondered. With all the leaning and pulling and kneeling, the only thing I managed to overstretch was a tendon in my knee.

I walked down to speak with my neighbor Jack. His son was there and as I told them proudly I was 'fixing fence' yet couldn't get the wire very taut, they laughed and kindly said, "What you need is a fence stretcher."

"Never heard of that, but I'll go buy myself one."

Luckily, in Wyoming, a fence stretcher is easily obtainable at any hardware store, and by just looking at the picture on the box cover, I could figure out how to employ it.

Wyoming Game and Fish has a guide on their website called *'How to Build Fence with Wildlife in Mind.'* Before I saw this guide, I got the notion that I'd change my entire fence to smooth, instead of barbed, wire. I hate barbed wire. I've torn many pants going over it, many shirts going under it, and it's hard to work with for obvious reasons. But I quickly found out that smooth wire alone won't keep cattle out.

Building a fence that all kinds of wildlife can handle, yet keeps livestock in, or out, is a creative endeavor. One has options, and has to tailor the fence to his needs. Fences can be four-strand or three, or of wood. A person needs to consider the movement of wildlife through his or her property; how they travel in different seasons and what kinds of wildlife are on your property. Pronghorn, which I don't have in my valley, but are down in the flats around Cody, will not go over a fence unless pushed hard by fear. They prefer to go under. The minimum bottom strand for them to crawl under must be 18″ from the ground. Not only is the bottom strand height important. Studies have shown that one ungulate (a hoofed animal such as a deer or elk) per year for every 2.5 miles gets tangled and dies due to fences, and 70% of those mortalities were on fences higher than 40 inches. One erroneous notion people have is that a fence with looser wires is safer for wildlife. This is completely not the case. When jumping a fence where the top wire isn't taut, a deer

Pronghorn trying to negotiate a fence whose bottom strand is too low

can too easily get a foot caught.

Buck and Rail, sometimes called Jackleg fences, were commonly used in this country in the past. They don't require digging post holes which is a plus in the Rocky Mountains. The previous owners installed a Jackleg fence along one side of my property and it's in good shape. Although they last for a long time, they can be difficult for wildlife, especially moose, to negotiate. I've watched a cow moose spend over a week teaching her yearling moose how to jump fences. Calf moose only stay with their moms for one year and this teenager was about to be kicked out of the nest. Mom wandered the large pastures across from my home with her calf in tow. She approached the first fence — a wire one — jumped it, crossed the dirt road, then cleared the buck and rail fence on the neighboring property. She strolled leisurely, without ever looking back, across the pasture several hundred yards to the forest edge. She waited,

Elk stuck behind a high fence trying to flee from wolves

partially hidden in the trees, and watched her calf. Meanwhile the yearling ran back and forth along the first fence line, scared to jump. He spent ten minutes looking for a way out, finally jumping at a low spot along the easement line, walked across the road and up my open driveway, then searched my buck-and-rail fence till he found the dropped rails I'd left for winter wildlife crossings. His roundabout way worked but took an exhaustive amount of time. Mom patiently waited and assessed her teenager's progress from afar, acting indifferent while remaining completely attentive. This cow moose's behavior was instructive for every parent of a teenager. Every few days she repeated this ritual until finally the calf started to get the idea. Jumping fence apparently was the last lesson mom needed to teach him before he was booted out on his own.

Fixing fence was a task I could learn sufficiently to do by myself. But there were others, more massive projects that needed professional skills. I began a remodel process as money permitted, slowly, over the next three years. I was loath to spend too much money as I still thought of the cabin as a place to crash between long backpack trips, or maybe a free get-away location for friends and family. Yet, while there were just some things that were unlivable — like that '60's orange shag carpet full of dirt and dust, or the windows that didn't open — there were other issues that were critical. The pre-sale inspector hadn't been able to find any evidence of a septic system such as a clean-out pipe, so it was left unchecked. However after the following spring when the ground thawed I found where the 'septic system' lay. There, in the front yard, was a large crater ten feet wide and six feet deep with a concrete box at the bottom. Now it was imperative I install a real septic and soon, before someone fell into that hole. And then there was the winter when the pipes burst that required the replumbing of the entire house. Money well spent but hard earned and going fast.

By October of the second year, I happened to be here during a big snow storm. It was then I realized that if I had to stay inside the cabin all day, or even for a few days, I better like where I was. That's when the unfinished rooms and the bulging old paneling started to get to me. I'd been coming enough times that the cabin was no longer just a go-between from California to the Wind River Mountains or Yellowstone. Now something else was calling me. In Wyoming, no remodel work gets down in the winter. My new plans would just have to wait till the following summer.

The spring of 2007 was the height of the housing boom. Carpenters in Cody had more work than they wanted, and none of them needed to drive two hours a day to redo my walls. I figured it was a two to three week job, but how could I accomplish this task? I decided to ask my Guatemalan foreman if he knew of any carpenters that needed work. It turned out his father, an accomplished carpenter, was coming to California from Guatemala on a six-week work visa. I hired his dad, Naples, and another carpenter, Noe, whom I knew from my crew, to come to Wyoming, stay at the cabin, and put blue-stain tongue and groove beetle killed pine on my walls. They, along with Noe's seven-year old son Kevin, arrived in their tiny Toyota truck, piled high with power and hand tools, a stove and all their food, and Kevin's bicycle.

When I returned to the transformed cabin in October, things were shifting for me. It had been a tough few years. My life was rapidly changing and I was exhausted, emotionally and psychically The deaths of my brother and his wife deeply troubled me. Almost fifteen and twenty years older than me, they'd filled a role as surrogate parents when I was younger. My foreman and friend had suddenly died that spring, leaving another big hole. Without my foreman's assistance, I'd taken on the task of managing his crews, while working long hard hours on a large and important installation for a prestigious garden tour deadline. And my parenting job as a single mom would soon change dramatically as my son approached college.

One day I hauled a chair to the high meadow of my property. I sat for several hours, watching the view, feeling the wind on my face, letting my thoughts run out. From this vantage I could see the entire valley. The massive abrupt Absarokas to my west and north, the ancient granitic Beartooths to the northwest. Encircled by high mountains, the forest alive with the wholeness of an intact ecosystem, for the first time in my life I understood what it meant to 'be centered.' I had found my center. It was here, inside of me and outside of me. For me, this place was the heart of the Universe, and when I was here, all things were right.

I returned to California a different person. I felt deeply healed. I found myself spending more time dreaming about Wyoming. I talked about it incessantly with my friends, who by now were bored with it; I longed to be there when I was away, and felt completely at peace and at home when I returned.

What my impulsivity didn't take into account was the practical side. I was now weighted down under the pressure of two mortgages, and all the improvements I had taken on. Most of the time I felt like my life was just about work and no play. I had to hustle constantly to get jobs, design and install them, and obtain new ones if I wanted to stay afloat. In addition, the divide between the atmosphere of Wyoming — its wide open spaces, the relaxed manner of its inhabitants, the wildness — and the crowds and manic pace I felt in the Bay Area was growing wider. My life just seemed out of sync, no longer a puzzle piece fit between California and myself.

One autumn day while working in my home office, I glanced outside to see the neighbor's cat on my fence. She was watching a hummingbird on a branch in the apple tree. The hummingbird was too far away for the cat to catch. I watched this dance for about five minutes, waiting to see what might happen. The cat, as cats do, remained patient and didn't move, stealthily eyeing his potential prey, while the bird nonchalantly sat on the limb. In a flash, the hummingbird flew directly towards the cat and into its' jaws. I was stunned. It was as if the cat had put a spell on the bird. Or was the bird committing suicide? That bird could have flown in any direction. He had not been in any danger where he was sitting. Yet instead, he had made a sacrifice of himself. Afterward one friend said, "No, it was the color of the cat. Or a shiny bell she was wearing. Was it an orange cat?" suggesting the cat, like a flower, had fooled the bird. But this cat, who I'd seen many times on that fence, was drab gray and had no bell. I was convinced it was some unseen and imperceptible attractive cat energy that drew the bird directly to him.

This odd occurrence disturbed me, but over time this same phenomenon, like an outward symbol, appeared to characterize the process that was taking place in my own life. I was being drawn to my property more and more, like a spell put on me, and that move would require a complete sacrifice of everything I had known all my life — my friends, my home, my job, and all that had anchored me in the past. Certainly for me, it was a kind of death, a spiritual or psychic death.

The hummingbird and the cat marked the beginning of a process of a new way of looking at life, beyond even the traditional "cycle of birth and death".

I had just begun to explore selling my home in California when

Soona was diagnosed with bone cancer. I like to think she knew she couldn't do this next journey with me. She was too worn out at thirteen and a half. The best advice I was given was to take off work and make her last week or two filled with everything she loved. I did just that, took her to the beach (her favorite thing as a Golden Retriever), bought her hamburgers at drive thru's, took her to the park, and gave her lots of petting and attention. Just the year before, Soona was diagnosed with an adrenal problem. The vet wanted to put her on a series of expensive medications and shots. Instead, I made the decision to buy a puppy. Koda was the best shot of medicine I could have given Soona. I was going to need a hiking companion in Wyoming and Soona was too old now for long treks. With another dog to compete with, Soona had come back to life. Koda gave her a good last year.

But now, Koda, the crazy and still naïve pup, seemed to know what was going on. He was comfortable playing second fiddle and didn't demand my attention. But when the two weeks were up, I balked. It was so hard. And Soona still was able to walk around enjoying the wind on her face. I knew that the vet said she'd need to be put down before the cancer killed her, because her pain would become unbearable over time. But she didn't display symptoms of being in pain. When was the right time? It was at that point that I had a series of intense and vivid dreams, dreams I almost felt were given to me by Soona, as if she were telling me she was ready. One of these dreams gave me the strength to take the next step, a dream filled with the imagery borne out of the wilds of Wyoming where my little cabin was awaiting me.

The dream took place in Yellowstone, where a group of wolf watchers crowded against a glass wall to watch a pack of wolves hunt down a large cow elk. Every person seemed fascinated by the wolves, without much attention to the prey. One person even brought in a bowl of water beyond the glass barrier for the wolves to drink from. But unlike everyone else, my own impulse in this dream world was to look directly into the elk's face, into her eyes. As she lay dying, I saw this cow elk was surrendered to her fate as a prey animal, and her impending death. There was no fear in her eyes.

There was powerful instruction here. My dream suggested the entire cycle needed to be taken together. You can't just be fascinated with the wolf, or sympathetic to the elk. Taken together, they are one. Otherwise, you will be 'cut off,' just observing part of the process from behind the glass, as if watching a movie. The elk needs the wolf as much as vice versa. I was so sympathetic with my connection to my 'wolf' — Soona — that I was blind to her own need to surrender into her death.

Strangely, the next morning after these dreams, I awoke to find Soona disoriented. She'd gone outside up some patio steps, unable to return. The time was now. Because Soona was afraid of the vet's office, I'd arranged for a vet to come to the house. His customary practice was to give the animal the lethal injection, then dispose of the body himself to save the owner the emotional pain. Once the animal was dead, he'd put it in his truck and leave for his next appointment, allowing little time for the owners to 'sit with the body.' But that felt too abrupt, even callous to me. I wanted to spend a little time with Soona's body after she was gone, so I asked if he'd just help me carry her 85 pound frame to my car. I stayed with her for a while, then drove her myself to the Humane Society for cremation. Though hard, it's only right that we allow ourselves to experience the whole process together with those we love, including our pets.

After Soona's death, all the old pieces of my life in California no longer fit. My son was away at college, my work partner was gone. I struggled with the idea of selling my home. I knew if I did that I'd never be able to afford to buy in California again. It was a major decision, a crossroads. The tipping point was a strong feeling that I couldn't shake: that the booming economy was going to take a dive within the next six months, and if I hesitated now, it could be another five or ten years before home prices bounced back. It was now or never. In early spring of 2008 I decided to begin 'staging' my home, a common selling practice in California.

By May when we listed the house, the market was already beginning to slow, but the economy had not yet collapsed. When an acceptable offer came through, the banks had begun to tighten up lending practices. The banks had seen the writing on the wall for months, yet the public was still in the dark. In order for the buyers to obtain their loan, they were told to push ahead. Our closing date was moved up a month, to mid-August, just a month before the Great Banking Collapse went public.

Everything was happening quickly, more quickly than I'd anticipated. I was in Wyoming when the final papers were signed. I raced back to California to clean out the old home, box what was going into storage, and pack my car with the items I wanted to bring to Wyoming.

I was moving to a much slower, more natural pace — from a season-less environment, where wet and dry were the only expressions of change in the natural world to a land with long winters, short shoulder seasons and compressed summers. In the modern and comfortable world we all live in, time is measured in hours, days, months, the number of emails we receive in a day and the fastness of our internet speed. Yet here in Wyoming time rolls along according to the sun and the moon. The town of Ten Sleep is from an Indian name meaning how many 'sleeps' it takes to walk from one Indian destination to another over the Big Horn Mountains. I was entering this new world of 'sleeps' and 'moons'.

The Crow Country is good country. The Great Spirit has put it exactly in the right place, while you are in it you fare well; whenever you go out of it; whichever way you travel you fare worse.

Crow Chief Rotten Belly

CHAPTER 3

The People Before

My first encounter with archaeological remains in the valley was, you could say, a tease, a false sign. My friend Don told me he'd heard of a wikiup up river somewhere. He described a vague location, telling me that his co-worker knew where this Indian dwelling was. A general term, a wikiup is a dwelling or hut with an oval frame of branches covered with brush or grass. In these parts, the Sheep Eater Indians made wikiups of large pieces of bark in a conical shape. So in my general scouting adventures I kept an eye out for this hut.

One afternoon I was tooling around off trail, following a creek upstream. On my return, I traipsed northward, wandering through a maze of dry arroyos. The forest opened up, a clearing appeared, and there, standing intact before me was the wikiup. I almost couldn't believe my eyes. I had no training in these matters yet this conical gathering of poles appeared authentic enough to be the real deal; it was well hidden and not on a trail. Outside the dwelling, on its northern face, someone had left a full set of antlers, an offering perhaps. The door faced east which is traditional. I had to crouch low to enter. It was small inside, only about 8' in diameter, but very comfy. The mosquitoes outside had been annoying me, but inside it was cool with no bugs.

The wikiup was in remarkable shape. From the little I knew, the native Sheep Eater Indians probably hadn't been around these parts since the establishment of Yellowstone Park in 1872. That's a long time for it to be in such good condition. But I was sure this was the one my friend had told me about.

Later while hiking with a friend, I crossed through the local dude ranch property. The owners had grown up around the area and knew a lot about its' archaeological sites. One of the sons had even done his college thesis on the Sheep Eater Indians. I asked about the wikiup.

"Oh, you found it. Good for you. Back about twenty-five years ago, one of our wranglers got real interested in the local Indians

An Authentic Sheep Eater Wikiup

and how they lived. He wanted to see if he could make a wikiup. He did a good job. It's still standing."

The real deal it wasn't, but it was a good beginning.

* * * * * *

My first May after the purchase, I drove down the county dirt road that ends five miles from the Park's boundary. Few visitors use the road at that time of year so it was unusual when I encountered a forest service truck.

"We're the caretakers at the Forest Service cabins," the couple in the truck told me.

I asked about all the important things I was dying to know — bears, hiking trails, things to see in the valley.

"There's supposedly a log sheep trap the dude ranch takes people to on trail rides. We've seen them head up and over that ridge."

They pointed to a low saddle that stretched out seemingly forever into wilderness area. Not much definition or direction for a greenhorn like me. I thanked them and kept that thought in my imaginary notebook.

The following year in 2007, I spent the month of October at the cabin. By now I'd heard the term Sheep Eater Indians several times, and I wanted to know more about these early inhabitants of this valley. I began my research at the local library, only to find a reference to another sheep trap, this one made of natural boulders. A friend of mine who I regularly hiked with had promised to take me to the sheep trap the caretakers told me about. So I concentrated on finding this second one.

It was fall and that meant hunting season. I decided I'd ask some local hunters if they knew the location of this natural trap.

Surely, I thought, with all their intricate knowledge of the back-country, they'd give me some direction. In mid-October, I was invited to a birthday party at a nearby ranch. Some of the guests had been hunting around these parts for over twenty-five years. I asked several of them about Sheep Eater traps or other Indian evidence.

"I have no idea. What are you talking about?" was the general response.

I'd then tell them the little bit I knew.

"There were Sheep Eater Indians who lived here, Shoshones, who hunted big horn sheep and made special wooden structures to trap them in."

Invariably, they'd all answer "Wow, I never heard of this."

These men who rode on horseback everywhere looking for deer and elk, into drainages and hanging valleys too rugged for me to even dream of exploring, had undoubtedly passed right by the pens many times. It was then I realized that although I had this wide raging thirst to eat up everything about this land, not everyone who lived, hunted or recreated here did.

* * * * * *

The Shoshone Indians are Numic speaking peoples. Their ancient roots can be traced to the Great Basin, and perhaps, along with other Numic speaking tribes, to an area east of the Sierra Nevada Mountains called the Owens Valley. It is believed they first arrived in Idaho and Wyoming approximately 4,000 years ago. Multiple migrations came afterwards.

The Shoshone bands referred to each other by what they ate. Richard Adams of the Wyoming State Archaeology Office explains, "Regional groups were named for the dominance of a particular food in the diet of that group and, while they were not formal political units and membership was flexible, they were tied to specific areas." So there were Salmon Eaters and Groundhog Eaters, Rabbit Eaters, Dove Eaters and Buffalo Eaters as well as Sheep Eaters. These sub-groups were fluid kin-cliques where inter-marriages took place.

One of the unique aspects of the Sheep Eaters is that they never adopted the horse. By 1730-1750 all tribes had access to horses. When Lewis and Clark arrived in southern Montana they met Shoshones who were highly skilled horsemen, and wanted to trade their horses for guns. Instead, the Sheep Eater Shoshones (sometimes referred to as the Mountain Shoshones) used dogs to carry their goods. For them, dogs presented a real advantage. Sheep Eaters hunted mountain bighorn sheep as their primary food, an animal that lives in high locations where horses cannot easily travel. Their dogs also helped with the hunt. Hunting bighorn sheep involved driving them between a 'V'-shaped driveline made of logs that ended in a pen, or trap. The pen's entrance was a ramp. The sheep entered, were crowded inside, then killed with clubs. The dogs could help corral the sheep towards the drivelines. In their high mountain homes, horses would need to be fed during the winter with the deep snows. Yet dogs could eat meat alongside their owners. Sheep Eaters so loved their dogs that they were fed first before they fed themselves. They made snow booties for their large wolf-like companions and buried them alongside their owners.

Mountain Shoshones were a secretive lot. Because they lived high up in difficult mountain terrain, they didn't need to do battle with adversaries or intruders. Their dogs alerted them to strangers, and then they could easily retreat into their craggy natural fortress.

Probably one of the first white men to encounter Sheep Eaters was Osborne Russell in Yellowstone in 1835 in the Lamar Valley. Russell observed:

"Here we found a few Snake Indians...who were the only Inhabitants of this lonely and secluded spot. They were all neatly clothed in dressed deer and Sheep skins of the best quality and seemed to be perfectly contented and happy."

A few decades later, with the discovery of gold and silver, miners as well as travelers going west began exhausting the supply of game, overfishing the streams and lakes, cutting down the forests, and polluting the rivers. With the introduction of domestic sheep, the native bighorn sheep began dying in droves from disease. All this as well as human diseases like smallpox, worked to erode the culture and population of the Indians. In the few subsequent sightings after Russell's, Sheep Eaters were described as 'dirty, destitute, primitive, sub-human.'

By the time Yellowstone was made into a national park in 1872, the Park's superintendent Philetus Norris, worked to move all native peoples onto the reservations. Sheep Eater Indians were banned from their homeland to provide tourists with a comfortable vacation.

Given that these Mountain Shoshone Indians relied on bighorn sheep not only for their food, but clothing and bows, I had to wonder what the sheep population used to look like in these mountains. Bighorn sheep have precarious immune systems. Even after over 150 years of intermingling, they've never built up resistance to domestic sheep diseases such as pneumonia. Bighorn sheep historic populations may have numbered over two million. But by 1900 their numbers dropped to only several thousand. Efforts to reduce

hunting, reintroductions, and decreased domesticated sheep grazing have all allowed the bighorns to make a precarious comeback.
Public grazing allotments where domestic and wild sheep com-
mingle still create huge problems for bighorns today. In the last
few years an intensive study of bighorn sheep was conducted in
my area. The Wyoming Game & Fish discovered the sheep follow
ancient migratory routes. Although the department maintains our
area contains a healthy population of approximately 500 sheep,
these are extremely low historical numbers. Here, in contrast, is
what Trapper Osborne Russell saw in 1835 in Yellowstone:

*"An eye could scarcely be cast in any direction around, above or below
without seeing the fat [bighorn] sheep gazing at us with anxious curiosity
or lazily feeding among the rocks and scrubby pines."*

This, invariably, must have been what the Sheep Eaters saw.

This must have been what the Sheep Eaters saw.

Yet Sheep Eaters were far from being the impoverished Shoshones the white settlers thought. Among the Shoshones, the Sheep Eaters were at the top of the pecking order. They ate lots of meat, were living closer to the sun, and most important, they were regarded as particularly powerful medicine people. Sheep Eater Indians gained these powers through fasting at specific rock art sites. While in a trance state, a little person, a *nynymbi*, came out of a crack in the rock and the seeker followed him back inside. Once within the rock, the supplicant encountered a pantheon of creatures — sky people, water people, or ground people — who gave him supernatural powers, outlining the conditions under which he could use these abilities. When the quest was over, the initiate was instructed never to forget what he saw.

Water ghosts, *pandzoavits*, inhabited the springs, creeks, lakes and hot springs. Amongst this array of spirits, one of the most powerful was Water Ghost Woman, Pa *waip*. Turtle is her assistant. Spirits of all the three altitudes — sky, ground and water people — could travel. Larry Loendorf, an archaeologist who is an expert on the Sheep Eaters, states:

The panzoavits, for example, not only were powerful enough to make the water in hot springs boil but they were thought to travel through an underground hydrological network linking geysers in Yellowstone Park to hot springs in places like Thermopolis, Wyoming. Other spirits traveled from lake to lake through interconnecting streams and rivers, while yet another group was able to move through rock formations using a system of connected fissures and caves. Despite their mobility, spirits had a home territory, and it was there that they were most likely to be encountered.

Through shamanistic harnessing of the powers of the hot springs and Water Ghost Woman, the Sheep Eaters were considered the most powerful of all the Shoshone bands.

The research I'd done at the library provided me a context as well as a small map of the natural boulder cleft trap site. Apparently, according to the map, the boulders were positioned near a heavily used game trail. The map was purposely crude so people couldn't locate it. The contour lines were only 30' apart instead of the usual 200'. This meant the map would portray a tiny area, which, in the vastness of this country, made it hard to pinpoint exactly where it was.

After all the puzzled looks from hunters, I decided I needed to find the answers on my own. I had a basic idea where to look from trying to overlay a larger scale map and match up the contour lines. I spent several weeks honing in on the area where an extensive series of meadows sat atop sheer bluffs. Below these massive walls was a deep canyon. A series of draws flowed from the high bench above to the canyon below. I assumed the game used these drainages as built-in easy passageways, so I explored each one of them. But in all that up and down over the course of weeks, I didn't find anything that fit the description of this natural boulder pen.

Fall was in full force and the days were short. Soon the snows would be too deep for exploring and I would be heading back to California. One afternoon I had an idea to try a different tact. I took a few hours and hiked the escarpment to the base of the cliffs, steep but doable. Then I followed the outline along the massive rock, exploring along its folds. The walls' irregular shape led to interesting discoveries. I stopped to investigate a natural arch and enjoy the view of the canyon from high up.

Farther along, I came to an extremely narrow notch. I was curious and the small slot seemed interesting. The light was getting low, I was running out of time, and this seemed like a sidetrack. But I couldn't resist. I scrambled on all fours through some snow up the narrow passageway to a small flat area above. Walking around on top of large rocks, I noticed a second but larger cleft between two gigantic boulders that led downhill. The boulders narrowed sharply with a tree growing at the base. It was an unusual formation. A few pieces of wood and debris were inside. I looked around but saw no evidence of any drive lines of old logs.

I climbed back down the notch and continued making my way along the wall. In short order I came upon a dry creek bed and a well used game trail that led to the same ledge I'd just come from. It was then that it hit me — that cleft WAS the pen, just a natural one. It was so obvious. I raced back up the ravine as the sun was starting to set. Sure enough, the game trail passed a few hundred feet above the rock crevice.

Cribbed Log Structure

And now I noticed random wood, very old logs, above the boulders, obviously once used as the drive line. I walked into the 'pen' itself and saw that the tree growing at the base was fairly young. But blocking the opening between the two boulders at the narrow end point was a large pile of old and weathered wood. This was not just a pile collected over time from storms. This was a deliberate 'fence' to prevent escape once the game had been corralled. The whole setup seemed so ingenious to me, with a minimal expenditure of energy. The ancient game trail right there, the Sheep Eaters waiting in the timber above, the natural pen below. From the valley far below where the present trail is, you'd never see or notice this area.

I sat down at the top of the rock and watched the setting sun. I marveled at how I'd found this place. It was getting cold now. I took a little time to sit and say 'thank you' to whatever helped me find this treasure of a place.

* * * * * *

George Frison is one of the premier archaeologists in Wyoming. He grew up in Ten Sleep, Wyoming, not far from here, and spent most of his life as a rancher, hunting guide, and avocational archaeologist. At the age of 37 in 1962, he went back to school to finish his undergraduate work in archaeology. By 1968 he was appointed the first Wyoming State Archaeologist. Because of his knowledge of the land as well as his hunting skills, he had a natural intuitive ability and understanding of what it took to survive for prehistoric peoples. He learned how to make and use darts and atlatls, and went to Africa to discover how prehistoric hunters in North America might have brought down mammoths. Frison experimented in Zimbabwe with modern Clovis points on African elephants that were being culled to get rid of excess numbers. He found that the Clovis tools were not only adequate, but very successful in penetrating the hide and ribcage of an African elephant, and quite possibly a mammoth as well. Frison's main passion was understanding the Paleoindian mammoth hunters. He was among the first to hypothesize that climate may have killed off the late Pleistocene megafauna, still an unresolved issue among researchers. He concedes that while there is little convincing evidence of Clovis hunters actually killing large extinct predators such as short-face bears or dire wolves, they may have hastened the demise of mammoths.

I purchased his massive *Prehistoric Hunters of the High Plains*, a virtual encyclopedia of the prehistory of Wyoming and southern Montana. In it I found references to a dig that was done at the Dead Indian site near my home.

A friend in town told me he was taking a night course with Larry Todd on local archaeology. Larry Todd had assisted on one of the digs with Frison in this valley in the '80's. A Wyoming archaeologist working as a professor at Colorado State University, Larry had recently retired from teaching and was devoting his attention to his own projects exclusively. It was deep winter and the hour drive to and from Cody for his class, at night, over an 8800' pass, would have been daunting. I asked Larry if I could audit his May field trip to the Dead Indian site instead. When May weather cancelled the trip. Larry graciously consented to give me an individual tour of Dead Indian. He was leading a middle school class field trip there and I could come afterwards.

Dead Indian is on the National Register of Historic Places. In the 1970's, when the road construction crew was initiating paving the old dirt road, the excavation discovered archaeological artifacts. The road work was halted and the dig began, overseen by George Frison. What emerged was a treasure trove — a picture of the native peoples living here continuously during the winter months for over 4500 years.

The people who lived at Dead Indian probably were the first Shoshones. The timing of occupancy coincides with the estimated first migrations. Going back 10,000 years, the biggest clues come from different styles of arrowheads. Between the time period of 5000 to 7500 years ago there is a dearth of archaeological evidence. This is known as the Early Archaic Period coinciding with the Altithermal. The Altithermal was an extended period of drought, which had a significant effect on the human and animal populations. Why there are so little archaeological remains from this period is still being debated, but the thought is that the local inhabitants moved to higher elevation sites to escape droughty conditions.

Dead Indian's historical occupancy spans over several archaeological time periods, but first usage shows up at the end of the Altithermal and the beginning of what's known as the Middle Archaic Period. This was a time when the climate eased, as bison began to reappear in the cultural remains of Plains Indian cultures. There is evidence of increased use of plant foods and more complex food preparation with the use of pit ovens. At Dead Indian, the peoples mostly ate deer and in smaller numbers, sheep. There is also extensive evidence of complex rituals involving deer worship.

Larry and I walked over to a large plateau as he painted a picture of a campsite with upwards of several hundred people, living in family groups–a small Wyoming town so to speak. I asked if they'd found tipi rings, those circles of rocks one sometimes finds in the desert that were used to hold down the skins covering a tipi.

"When we excavated in the 70's, there were formations that looked like pit houses, but no one had ever seen those kinds of dwellings this far north, so the notion was dismissed. But since then we've verified that, yes, there were pit houses."

People living in these pit houses, came here winter after winter to hunt the game that was plentiful. These native peoples followed nomadic yet predictable routes. In the spring, they probably followed the game to the grasses higher up. They also needed to retool and for that they needed new stone material. They had their favorite summer hunting and quarry locations, while they wintered down at these lower elevations.

In this early Archaic period, the big game were still scarce, and more intensive hunting and gathering was necessary for the equivalent quality of nutrition. People were settling down for longer periods and returning to the same sites. The Dead Indian site was like a novel, with many chapters. Larry suggested Dead Indian might have gone through periods of heavy and lighter use. Having been occupied continuously for so long, probably many different periods of histories and stories had taken place here.

As we walked around the site, Larry bent down and showed me how almost every square inch, to the trained eye, contained evidence of habitation. Chippings from chert, quartzite, chalcedony, pieces of bone, a sheep vertebrae–all this he found within a few square feet. I hadn't seen any of this until he pointed it out.

We walked back to the road while Larry told me a story about bison, his specialty. He said that Native Americans didn't always use all the meat. It was common to just take the prime parts after a kill. One time, accompanied by one of his students, he was talking with a Blackfoot elder about ancient hunting methods. When he came to the part about how they left parts of the kill, a student listening nearby said,   "They wasted parts?"

"Would you take all of it?" asked the elder. "Would you be that greedy?"

The student replied, "I wouldn't waste anything. I'd take it all."

"You whites are so greedy," said the elder. "You wouldn't leave any meat for your brothers–the wolf, coyote, raven."

Larry ended our meeting by stressing the importance of protecting these special places. "So many archaeological sites are looted, treasures are stolen. You're living here and being interested in this is good. Keep a watch on the Sunlight area."

I told him I would and thanked him for his time.

After that first visit, from time to time I come back to the Dead Indian site and sit. At the bend in the road, where the bridge runs over Dead Indian Creek, I walk paralleling the river to the flat sagebrush clearing where the main dig was. Bordering one side of this clearing, and twenty feet down, is the creek. Over the course of 5000 years, the creek has eroded the channel down that low. I try to envision how the creek probably was nearer the height of the now vanished pit houses.

On the opposite side of the main Indian campsite, to the southeast, is a high steep wall. To the south is the trail leading down Dead Indian's wide valley, a route to the higher passes and steep mountains of the Absarokas. There is a plateau overlooking the main campsite. A magnificent enormous erratic boulder, looking very out of place, stands solitary here, surrounded by sage and death camas (*Zigadenus venenosus*). Were lookouts stationed up here to guard the camp? Did the children play up here? I imagine they did and while I close my eyes and listen hard, I can't hear their voices. From this vantage above the meadow, you can view across to a notch between two prominences. It's a pass for deer, elk, wolves and coyotes. Sometimes, on sunny winter days I sit near the large boulder and watch small bands of elk moving through the higher meadows beyond the campsite. Across the creek to the north, a summit in the shape of a steamboat sports multiple tiers of flat grassy areas, a haven for the elk in winter when strong winds expose the forbs and grasses.

The peoples living here had been masters of observation when it came to animals. They lived in sympathetic intimacy with them. They respected them, told stories about them, called upon them to be available for the hunt which provided their sole source of protein as well as hides for clothing and other practical uses. Animals weren't lesser or lower beings, but were viewed as direct representatives of the spirit world, vehicles of spiritual communications and powers.

According to Frison:

"This respect is manifest through proper ritualistic treatment of dead animals...If there is one thing that separates present-day sport hunting from prehistoric hunting at a subsistence level, it is this lack of respect for the animals and the resulting proscriptions placed on procurement."

Frison describes the unusual discovery of ceremonial use of deer at this site. *"Deer were taken in considerable numbers throughout the winter, and several large male skullcaps* [meaning antlers with top of skull attached] *were given unusual treatment. One was placed in a hole in the center of a rock cairn and others were placed to one side of it. At least two of the specimens are large enough to be regarded as trophies today."*

Because deer were the main source of food at this site, they were highly venerated and used ritually, contemplatively. Deer were a totem or stair-step to another consciousness and by honoring them, respecting them, calling upon them, they would make themselves available to the people when the hunt came.

During the end of the Altithermal period, animal populations were just beginning to rebound. Deer must have been easier to find and kill than bison or sheep, thus a most important source of meat. Even today mule deer are the most abundant ungulate year-round in these mountains. Everyone in North America, even city-folk, is familiar with deer. In suburbs throughout the United States, they come into the yards and eat our cultivated garden plants. Deer are the most hunted animal in the United States, a multi-billion dollar sport.

Yet since moving here, I've had the most interesting experiences with deer that make me wonder more deeply about their nature, rather than see them just as pests or prey.

I was living full time in Wyoming, but continued for several years to do winter design work, November through January, in California to make ends meet. Upon my return one winter, I was beginning to open up the cabin. It's always a big process. I have to turn on the water, electricity, pump, and get the house heated up when it's below freezing outside. My friend Gary had come to help with the process. I'd met Gary when he built a fence for my neighbor. He lived in town but watched over their property. I needed help with cutting and hauling firewood, and Gary, a retired forest ranger, was the man for the job. Over time, he had helped me burn slash piles, installed new bathroom cabinets, and built an outhouse for the upper cabin. Working together, we'd become good friends and today he brought along his dog, so we had two dogs.

We were inside, tending to the business of the cabin, when the dogs outside started barking. It was the kind of bark that means there's wildlife around. Koda knows not to run after deer, but when he's in a pack (and two dogs constitute a pack mentality), I have to watch him. Gary and I walked outside. The dogs were barking towards the woods. At first we saw nothing and couldn't understand what was causing the dogs' agitation. Then, after we'd quieted the dogs, a large buck came out of the trees and started making his way across the meadow. The snow was soft and deep. We assumed the buck was heading east, away from the cabin. The four of us — two humans and two dogs — watched in silence as the buck walked slowly, deliberately, and regally through the deep snow. The depth of the snow almost made him look wounded as he walked. We stared in amazement as this large buck walked across the meadow, through my gate and into my front yard. He stopped about ten feet directly in front of us. The dogs were quiet. I think, like us, they were mesmerized. Here was the Deer King. He stood before us with his full beautiful rack. His large eyes stared directly into ours for a long time, at least a full two minutes. I wasn't sure if I should bow or run. Then just as he had come, he turned and slowly walked away. He was done with us.

Another incident occurred one early July morning. I heard a ruckus coming from the woods. A crashing and banging through the trees, so loud, I thought it might be a bear. But shortly a young buck emerged, walked to the top of the rise above the cabin, and stood looking directly at me for a few moments. Then he took off and disappeared. Around noon I stepped outside and noticed a large shape, like a rock, up near the same spot where the deer stood earlier. I clambered up the hillside and there, lying dead, was the buck. He looked healthy enough and hadn't become caught in the barbed wire fence. He'd just walked over and died. The only thing I could see wrong was a small amount of blood coming out of his eye. I called the Game Warden. Chronic wasting disease is a concern here and a dead buck in the middle of the summer, obviously not killed by a predator, would be something he'd want to know about. Chris, our Warden, examined the buck yet to him as well, the deer looked healthy. He certainly didn't have chronic wasting, and there were no other marks on his body. Chris hauled the deer away so as not to attract grizzly bears with the summer homes close by. I was left to ponder this unusual death. I wondered if the buck was having problems seeing or possibly a dizziness or head trauma. Indeed, he was crashing through the woods, unlike how deer ordinarily move. But I also had the distinct feeling this buck was asking me for help. I once had a cat that ran away for months at a time. He liked to hang out with the neighborhood feral cats. But one day I came home from work, unexpectedly at noon, to retrieve something. There he was, lying half dead at my bedroom door. I hadn't seen Petey in over four weeks, but now when he was in trouble, he knew where to come. Although I had no direct relationship with this buck, I felt he, like Petey, had returned for my help.

These two deer experiences and others over time awakened me to their ethereal nature. Their grace and heightened sensitivity to movement and sound are a window into a consciousness altogether different than ours. It is no wonder that the native peoples in my valley honored them with prayer and ceremony, holding them in high esteem, not just for their meat, but as a spirit window, a doorway to another dimension.

As I continued exploring my new environs, I had come across a lightly used dirt road where I'd found obsidian flakes. I was curious about the general topography of the area — might it had been an ancient campsite or a hunting trail? On a nice summer day I took the time to walk the nearby stream and its adjacent meadows.

On the way back to the car along the service road, I noticed where cattle had forced some grass to dislodge along the uphill side of the road cut. I sensed something unusual and bent down to look. A stone with an odd surface was sticking out of the wall of dirt. I pried the stone from the exposed hillside. A four-inch knife of green chert, very finely crafted, fell into my hand. I'd never found an arrowhead or any Indian artifact before. And I especially never expected to find something as beautiful, as large, and as special as this spear point.

I contemplated what to do. Leave it in place or take it. Although it had been buried for probably two thousand years, six inches below the present grade, now that a cow's hoof had churned it up, it surely wouldn't last if I left it — in short order an ATV or even a cow could run it over and break it. I thought no more about it and pocketed it.

I drove home, still reeling from my discovery. I had recently hired a bobcat to smooth out some of the rough edges on a secondary road that climbs steeply behind the property. I thought I'd walk up there, check out the finished work, and contemplate all that had just occurred. A few steps behind the main house, I noticed another unusual piece of rock on the road. A small obsidian arrowhead that had been dislodged from all the earth moving work. Now, in just one afternoon, I'd found two arrowheads. It felt more dreamlike than real. Just the previous night I'd had a powerful, impressive dream that appeared to foreshadow these events:

I was in my childhood home. My mother (who had died about fifteen years before) was looking out our second story window onto the front walkway to our house. I walked over and said, "What are you looking at?" I stood beside her and I too looked onto the walkway. It was a moonless night and I saw endless lines of ghosts walking towards my front door.

"What do they want?" I asked her.

I looked out the window again. Now I stood alone, without my mother. She had moved to stand next to my father who had just entered into the room. Everything looked like an ordinary night, no ghosts.

I commented, "They're gone."

My mother walked over. With her by my side, I looked out the window and I could see the hordes of ghosts once more. I asked my mother to teach me to 'see'.

She said, "You can't learn to see. You are either born with it or not. You can only learn how to use it once you have it."

The scene abruptly changed and I was beside a man. He was looking for something old and buried. He was digging in the dirt near a culvert.

I said, "That's only thirty years old. You won't find it there as it's not old enough."

Without warning, the culvert was exposed and an underground staircase appeared. He went down the stairs. I asked if I should come too; he said, "No need to."

In reality, my mother, in her youth, had been known around the neighborhood as a bit of a psychic. She'd intuited the death of her aunt in Europe before her mother received the news, and she'd told me about other premonitions that came true. When she married and went into business alongside my father, her natural powers receded. Several years previously I had met a Shoshone man who told me these mountains were 'a dreamtime place'. As I thought about the synchronicity of my dream the night before, I realized it had been premonitory, that when I found these arrowheads, I literally contacted the ghosts of the past that lived here.

I'd been communicating with Molly, the Forest Service

archaeologist, regarding our little woods that were part of a proposed vegetation management plan. I told her about my knife and upon seeing it she was very excited and wanted to know where I had found it. She had to make sure the site wasn't scheduled to be included in the treatment areas.

"I'd like to bring Larry Todd out here and make a mold of that knife. That is a very unique and special find."

I told her that would be great and we arranged another date to walk to the site.

It's a long trip up here, so when Molly returned with Larry they planned to survey several sites along with making the mold. One of the sites included wikiups, which had been photographed and documented in the 1970's by the Forest Service. They intended to update those records, using modern GPS equipment. Molly pulled out a rough photograph and map from the original documentation. It clearly showed five standing wikiups, quite similar in appearance to the replica I'd encountered years before, but in much disrepair. I knew the trail well. I'd been on it several times, yet never seen anything like what I saw in the picture. Molly told me a long time resident of the valley remembered family picnics around these wikiups.

I led the way. Really, the trail was a cow track up a side gully. We arrived at a small clearing where the trail split between two distinct draws. It didn't take Larry more than a few moments to recognize the dwellings. To me they looked like piles of old logs strewn on the ground. He examined the wood and announced they were three or four hundred years old. It had been only thirty years since that photograph was taken and the wikiups were in fair condition. What had happened? The family who enjoyed picnicing here told Larry that the Forest Service had allowed a large ranch owner to graze his cattle on this stretch of forest; the cattle loved to rub against the standing logs and lie beneath their shade. I thought back to Larry's admonition about vandalism. This vandalism was being done by the Forest Service itself! They knew about these dwellings and they'd approved the area for grazing. I was appalled at the policies that unconsciously allowed these cattle to run rampant over native heritage sites. I think Larry was taking it as par for the course; he'd seen more than his share of vandalism and things much worse than this.

As time was running short, we left the opportunity to explore a nearby cave for another day and went back to the cabin to make a mold of the chert knife. Larry pulled out a small piece of soft clay material and pressed my stone point into it. The fact that Larry had chosen to make a clay replica of the spearhead for the University of Wyoming, instead of asking me for the original, was a gift that suggested reciprocity — the power of the knife for my vigilant protection of these sites. I asked Larry if he could tell its age.

"It's difficult because the very bottom has been broken off. I'd say 2500 years. This is a good spearhead and probably was inadvertently dropped by a hunter. This large of a piece wouldn't have been tossed off. It would have been reworked into a smaller piece."

The smaller obsidian arrowhead was more intact. Just the tip had broken. Larry aged it at 4000 years old based on its style and form. Truly, these were ghosts come knocking at my door.

* * * * * *

Sheep Eater Shoshones weren't the only Indians who used this area to the east of Yellowstone. This was once Crow country. The Crow came to this area over 500 years ago, in several waves. There were Mountain Crow and River Crow. The Mountain Crow used the Absarokas for vision quests, hunting, and plant gathering. I've found several sites in the valley that Larry Loendorf thinks are related to Crow Indians, such as vision quest rock circles and cribbed log structures used as temporary shelters.

These two groups, Crow and Shoshone, cohabitated this area peacefully. But unlike the Sheep Eaters, the Crow were a horse culture who hunted bison as their main source of protein. And no animal is more clearly etched in our consciousness with early American peoples than the iconic bison.

In 1931, Pretty Shield, a Crow woman born in the 1850's, shared her memories and stories with Frank Linderman, a writer who had earned a trusted reputation amongst the Crow. Pretty Shield was regarded as a healer and a woman of power, a powerful force in her community and family. Her story is special because it chronicles a transitional period from the days of hunting bison and living free, to settling on the reservation. In one narrative, Pretty Shield relates an account from when she was nine years old. The Crow camp was moving to another spot, and young Pretty Shield and some friends were dallying. They stopped for a swim in the river, spent time drying out their dresses, and now were far behind the moving camp. Trying to catch up with their village, one younger girl had a slow mare and was far behind. Pretty Shield offered to change horses with her as she felt a responsibility to look after this younger girl. The other girls had already traveled far ahead and as the two girls reached a hill, they saw their village moving east, and a large herd of bison moving north. They'd soon be trampled at the pace they were moving. Pretty Shield called to the young girl to ride as rapidly as she could. But Pretty Shield, on her friend's old mare, was having trouble racing ahead of the herd.

"A buffalo herd travels straight. Nothing turns it. This was a big herd, narrow in front, and very wide behind; and it was running. If I rode back, or stayed where I was, it would sweep me along with it. I saw that there was only one thing to do, and this was to ride across in front of it, as the other girls had done.

I whipped that old white mare till my arm ached. But it did little good. She could not make it. When the big herd closed around me I did not expect to see my people again.

The old mare turned to run with the buffalo. She had to; and I let go of my rope to hang onto the pack with both hands. I could hear nothing above the roar of the pounding hoofs, could see nothing in the blinding dust as the old mare, pushed this way and that way, raced on with the buffalo. I saw that they were passing us, that they were going faster than we were, but with such a herd as this one was I knew that the old mare would die long before the tail-end reached us. If she stumbled in the dust, if she stepped into a badger-hole, if she fell, we should both be trampled into bits too small for even a magpie to notice. I wondered if my rope might be dragging. If it were down, and dragging, the buffalo would surely step on it, and then we should fall.

The old mare began to slow up, finally stopping so suddenly that I went over her head, Swow!

I was so frightened that I had not noticed my father who, pressing his good buffalo-horse, worked us, the old mare and me, out of the herd. A man whose Crow name was Pecunnie roped the old white mare as soon as my father had worked her near enough to the herd's edge to be safe."

Bison hold something ancient and magnificent, a vision that opens up the soul to the living past. Once bison roamed all of North America, from northern Mexico even down to Northern Florida. They filled the land from the Rocky Mountains to the Mississippi, and in fewer numbers almost to the Atlantic Ocean. They lived at sea level, on the high plains, and above timberline. Whole cultures for thousands of years depended upon them for food, clothing, shelter and tools; they were the lifeblood of the country. General estimates run between thirty and sixty million bison in North America when the white man came. In Montana, Wyoming and Colorado alone, five to ten million.

Horace Greeley estimated, "I know a million [buffalo] is a great many, but I am confident we saw that number yesterday...[they] could not have stood on ten square miles." Reports of bison taking five days to pass a given point estimated one herd at four million. Trails eighteen miles wide with "that whole distance being trod to finest dust to the depth of six inches" were seen. Larry Barsness in *The Compleat Buffalo Book* writes "Thomas Farnham wrote that when traveling along the Arkansas fifteen miles a day, and able to see for fifteen miles on each side of the trail, in three days he'd seen about 1350 square miles of land entirely covered with buffalo...at about twenty animals per acre, we find that Farnham would have seen a mind-boggling seventeen million buffalo in three days."

Now there are only around 5000 genetically pure bison left, mostly in Yellowstone National Park.

Sometimes I drive to Lamar Valley in Yellowstone, an hour from my home, just to sit and watch them. The bison are the only animal in the Park that isn't in the valley where I live. Some primal part of me lifts up in recognition at the sight of bison — a prehistoric memory that cattle do not evoke. Because bison can carry a disease — elk can as well — called brucellosis that may cause cattle to abort, they are confined to the Park. Brucellosis is spread by a cow ingesting the afterbirth of an infected animal.

Only pregnant female bison in their first calving cycle after exposure to the disease have the possibility of shedding infected material in the environment. Brucellosis bacteria also degrades quickly in warm weather and exposure to sunlight; in addition predators in the environment quickly consume afterbirth. Yet because of this ever so slim chance of exposure to cattle, bison are not allowed to roam. The Department of Agriculture gives states a 'brucellosis-free' stamp of approval. Brucellosis will never be eradicated in the Greater Yellowstone Ecosystem because elk are primary carriers who are allowed to roam as they please. A simple solution would be for the Department of Agriculture to allow an exception for the GYE.

In hard winters, bison have the instinctual need to leave the Park for lower elevations to feed. Hundreds try to head for the northern range, but they are herded back into the Park and sometimes slaughtered by Park Rangers. All this because the cattle industry in Montana makes a big stink — even though in winter the bison are not calving and most of these public lands are not grazed by cattle. According to The Buffalo Field Campaign, an organization that works to stop the slaughter of Yellowstone bison, studies have shown that the relatively few herds of cattle that do graze in spring and summer could be easily managed by appropriate stocking dates that do not conflict with the winter bison range. Obviously, brucellosis is the cover for a larger issue. That is the fear of the cattle industry, cattle ranchers, losing their grazing rights on public lands, a feeling of entitlement to all the grass, public and private. There are even several ranchers who have said publicly they'd welcome bison on their property in the winter and are not concerned about brucellosis. The irony of all this is that cattle are the ones who transmitted the disease to the bison back in 1917 while grazing together in confined areas in the Park.

* * * * * *

The evidence that bison roamed this valley for thousands of years surfaces from time to time. My third winter in Wyoming the snows were deeper than usual and the run-off was high; I found an old partial skull. Several neighbors that year found full skulls — horns, teeth and all — in riverbeds exposed by the fast waters.

This ebb and flow of climatic conditions and wildlife over thousands of years required creative lifestyle changes and strategies on the part of the people living here to survive. Story, ritual, spiritual tradition, community — all needed to survive in this harsh climate for more than twelve thousand years. Studying the history of my area and encountering native sites added not only a richness to my experience, but I also began to formulate the question "what is a right relationship to the land?" and ponder it in greater depth.

"We reached the old wolf in time to watch a fierce green fire dying in her eyes. I realized then, and have known ever since, that there was something new to me in those eyes — something known only to her and the mountain. I was young then, and full of trigger-itch; I thought that because fewer wolves meant more deer, that no wolves would mean hunters' paradise. But after seeing the green fire die, I sensed that neither the wolf nor the mountain agreed with such a view."

Aldo Leopold

CHAPTER 4

Close Encounters of the Wolf Kind

It was summer and my first landowners' meeting. A good place to start when you know no one. Unlike where I was living in California, this was a landowners, not homeowners, meeting. In California I'd been chairing a landscape committee and after attending a few of the monthly regular homeowner meetings, I completely swore them off. A small usual crowd of rabble-rousers, complainers and know-it-alls consistently showed, reliably arguing every issue brought before the Board.

But the once a year landowners' meeting was a social event first, an opportunity to listen to a few professionals speak such as the Game Warden or the Fire Marshall, and lastly a little bit of business. Hot dogs and hamburgers were on the house, while the rest was potluck.

When the eating was done, a Forest Service employee gave a talk on the beetle situation. He had a blown up poster of an actual photo taken in the 1890's looking up the valley. Next to it, there was another poster of a photo taken this year. The fire suppression policy of the last century had led to an overgrowth of pines, old pines, now subject to beetles due to drought and old age.

Next, Mark Bruscino, the Game & Fish grizzly expert gave us strategies for living in a grizzly/human interface habitat. We talked about the 'bad' grizzlies that were dropped off at the end of the valley.

"These are bears that have gotten into trouble, usually with livestock. I'm here to tell you that these are the bears you least have to worry about. Bears have strong homing instincts, a desire to return to familiar country even if they are transported hundreds of miles away."

Mark gave us a phone number where we could obtain bear-proof trashcans and told us the government subsidized these expensive cans so we only have to pay $50 for one. "They can be the key to saving a bear's life, and maybe saving yours."

Finally a student doing her master's thesis on wolves in the area gave a short talk. Her name was Abby and she was out to meet the landowners in the area. We'll probably run into her over the next two summers, she said. She'll be collaring wolves in the spring, then tracking their movements over the summer and fall. The central theme of her thesis was predation and she would be documenting the amount of cattle predation in the area.

Afterwards I introduced myself to her and asked if she needed any help.

"If you like to hike, then you can help out by hiking to GPS coordinates where wolves have been."

Whatever it was, it sounded great, a chance to work with the wolves in the valley in some shape or form, plus get some good science along with it. We exchanged numbers and I told her I'd be back in the early fall.

When I returned to the valley in September, there were no messages from Abby. I finally got a hold of her by phone. "I finished my survey early because all my interns left and I needed to go back to classes. But next summer and fall I'll be here through October, with hopefully more collared wolves I can study."

* * * * * *

In the summer of 1997, newly separated from a 23 year marriage I was raising my eight-year-old son. Struggling emotionally and financially, I was grateful when my friend Tara asked if my son and I would like to accompany her family on a trip to Yellowstone where her older son had a summer job. We flew to Salt Lake City, rented a car and drove the seven-hour trip to Jackson Hole.

Backpacking throughout my teenage years had given me confidence in my survival skills. The last time I'd been in Jackson, which was the first and only time I'd been to Yellowstone, was the summer between high school and college. In the early 1970s, Jackson was a small Wyoming town. My friends and I spent time in Glacier, and two weeks hiking the backcountry of the Tetons. When we emerged from the wilderness, one of my companions became seriously ill, probably with food poisoning. A concerned adult at Gros Vente campground suggested we take Karen to the nearby forty-bed hospital and gave us a ride there. Karen was immediately given a bed and an IV, but since we other two girls had no where to go, and we 'thought' we were a bit sick too, the staff admitted all of us. We'd been on the road, hitchhiking and backpacking for two months, so a hot shower and a bed was a wonderful thing. The small hospital had only one other patient; its nurses treated us like royalty. We spent three glorious days as patients in this local Jackson Hole hospital.

I must have been living in a time warp since then, because I'd told Tara and her husband Steve that Jackson was small, and we wouldn't need a hotel reservation. When we got to Jackson I was in for a big surprise. By 1997, it had become a huge town of 12,000 people, catering to the yuppie, tourist and ski crowd. Our group, on the other hand, consisted of three adults and two eight-year-olds. Even Motel 6 was full at $100/night. We were lucky to find a room.

Since my friends' son, Chris, worked in Yellowstone, he was able to arrange a special treat for his family — the use for one night of a Patrol Cabin along Nez Perce creek. Although there's a service road leading to the cabin, we were required to hike in with our gear. The plan was for Chris and his family to use the cabin while I stayed with my son in a hotel in West Yellowstone. The one room cabin just didn't have enough beds for all of us. But at the last minute, Tara and Steve decided they would rather have a night on their own at the hotel and asked if I would go with Chris and the kids.

We set out on a perfect August day through a large meadow full of hot springs and cold springs. Every so often we'd test one of the hot springs. Finally we discovered a hollow where two streams met, one cold, the other hot. The temperature was perfect. The kids, Chris and I had a blast playing in the warm waters.

By the time we arrived at the patrol cabin, dusk was settling in. We made dinner in the small cabin, told stories and went to bed. I arose the next morning early. Chris was dressed and outside chopping wood for the next visitors. The kids were asleep. This was my chance for a short walk before breakfast.

I headed up the service road into a sparse lodgepole pine forest to see where the road led and emerged from the trees into a clearing. In the middle of a spacious meadow sat a large circular pen, over 100′ in diameter. The enclosure was chain link fence, at least ten feet tall. Inside the pen, circling at a fast run, were wolves, many of them. The wolves were running around and around the inside edge of the fence. In the stillness of a Yellowstone morning, far from traffic and human noises, all I could hear were the heavy sounds of the wolves panting as they circled their enclosure.

I took the scene in and at once knew that I had stumbled upon a place off-limits to the public. Their power and presence, energy and passion, was the most amazing sight I'd ever seen. In mid-January of 1995 several groups of wolves had been captured in Canada, then re-introduced into various pens in Yellowstone. I'd read about this, but didn't know the details, only that the wolves had been held in acclimation pens for a period of several months, then let free into the Park. The releases all had taken place in the early spring. So this couldn't have been part of those original reintroductions. In those first years, wolves that had gotten into trouble outside the Park with livestock were put back into pens. I wasn't clear who exactly these wolves were nor why they were here, but it was clear that I was privy to something extraordinary and very special. And I knew whatever was going on, the biologists in charge probably didn't want the wolves to have a lot of human contact, so I kept my distance. I watched for only a few moments, not wanting the wolves to catch wind of me.

Those wolves and their sighting may have marked the beginning of my transition to Wyoming. I went back to the patrol cabin, made breakfast, walked out to meet the rest of the group, and never said a word to anyone about what happened. There was something sacred as well as taboo in my sighting.

That same vacation, I'd arranged for my friends to fly home with my young son, while I fulfilled a promise I had made to myself on that trip long ago after high school. During that summer of

1972, after we emerged from our stay at the Jackson hospital, we picked up a ride where the driver asked, "Have you girls been to the Wind Rivers?" He told us that we just *had* to go and drove us all the way to a trailhead. We stayed and hiked for five days but never made it as far as the Continental Divide. I could see the immense rugged peaks of the Divide in the distance and vowed to come back someday. Now, broken from my recent separation, relieved for a week of the responsibility of my son, here was my chance. I also looked at it as a place to possibly heal from my grief and confusion.

I rented a car and went off to Big Sandy trailhead. In Jackson, the headlines were all abuzz with a missing woman. Amy Bechtel from Lander had taken her car, parked by a trailhead in The Sinks, and gone out for a run. She hadn't been seen for two days. Foul play was suspected. I was nervous. The Sinks and Big Sandy might be considered close by Wyoming terms. Separated by maybe one hundred miles, one on the south-eastern slopes of the Winds, the other on the south-western slopes, with only South Pass in between. I wasn't afraid to backpack on my own. I was a pretty experienced camper. And I wasn't afraid of animals — but crazy men running around the backcountry killing women was another story. Maybe this wasn't a good idea, I thought.

The road to Big Sandy trailhead is a lonely twenty miles. It travels across isolated federal and private ranch lands. It's easy to never see a soul or another car. That was the part that worried me, as well as the trailhead itself. I figured that if I could begin hiking and get in the five miles to the lake, any abductor would be too lazy to hike that far and I'd be safe! Needless to say, I made the trip into Big Sandy lake and the famous Cirque of the Towers. As for Amy Bechtel, her body was never found. Not a trace and no clues.

The wolves, the Winds — powerful icons planted in my heart

that pressed on me to return. The trip not only provided me the beginnings of the healing and comfort I needed, but the passion to make that trip every year for the next eight summers back into the Winds. Eventually I hiked the entire spine called The Highline Trail. The Winds became my spiritual home and refuge. Sometimes I stayed in Yellowstone, but always I'd return to the Winds.

* * * * * *

The first extended trip to my new home was for two weeks in early May 2006. I'd never even had a chance to drive beyond my house towards the end of the valley. I was excited to take my first hike. With snow still in most of the country, I met a ranger on the road and asked where I could find a good trail. He suggested the trail at the only campground in the valley.

"Black. He was black."

At the trailhead parking area, I met the former Game Warden who was returning with a small group from a trail ride. He told me there was a wolf den high up the trail. I took his advice and left Soona in the car.

"Doesn't she need bear spray?" one of the horseback riders asked, looking at me. My first trek here, I wasn't too schooled in the use of bear spray, which is pepper spray in a large canister, so I wasn't carrying any.

"She'll be alright." The Game Warden knew these parts well. "There's no bears out yet."

I started up the trail that led through thick forest for a mile, then opened up along a creek. I noticed a very large cave entrance high up at the base of the cliffs. The area had a special, almost sacred feel to it. Still early, not yet quite spring, a silence covered the land.

The warden had told me to head up towards the left for a great view. When I arrived at the confluence, where two canyons converged, several routes presented themselves. Trails are sparse here, maintained only by animals or horse traffic, I wasn't sure where to go or what to follow. What I didn't know was that I'd already missed the turn he suggested. Confused I took the first drainage, a gradual uphill along a dry creek bed, and a faint outline of a trail. A sign said:

Caution. Live Traps. Gray wolves are being trapped in this area for televelocity radio collars. The traps are leg traps. If you see a wolf in a trap do not attempt to release it. Even a leashed dog would be attracted to the bait. Report any trapped wolves immediately.

The trail is surrounded by cliffs on one side, and a gentle rise on the other. Sparse pines and aspens line the sides of the trail.

Today was a typical blustery spring day — threatening to snow — the sun peaked through the cloud cover every so often. To the West lay the magnificent Absarokas, the volcanic peaks of Yellowstone's northeastern border.

I walked up the narrow draw. Soon it opened into an immense marshy meadow with an old horse corral. I could see the meadow broaden significantly higher up, and beyond lay a thick forest. I knew Soona would be wondering when I'd be returning. I pulled out an energy bar, sat down to ponder how I'd feel if I were to actually see a wolf. The warden did say there was a den somewhere up here. Surely they'd be wary around their den. I figured I'd be afraid.

I packed up and began the return hike, using a trail slightly higher up. The sound was what startled me. It was a different earth sound than I was used to — either in California or from the granite floor of the Winds. This was a hollow *thump*. Maybe it was because the ground was still frozen. Maybe because of the limestone base, but the thump made me look up. There, ahead of me about twenty feet, was a large black wolf. He trotted uphill off the trail; now he was standing above and ahead of me, twenty-five feet away. He turned his head and stared at me. We exchanged a wordless gaze for what felt like an eternity. I fumbled for my camera, but he was gone. No, I hadn't been afraid at all.

Months later at a winter wolf watching excursion in the Park, I met Doug Smith, Yellowstone's wolf biologist.

"I doubt you saw a wolf," he said when I told him of my wolf experience. "It was probably a coyote. That's too chance and up close an encounter."

I didn't blame him for doubting me. I listen to people in Yellowstone all the time making the same mistake. But I knew I'd seen a wolf. I've seen many coyotes and this was not one.

"What color was he?" Doug asked.

"Black. He was black."

"Then you saw a wolf," he confirmed.

* * * * * *

In August of 2008, nine months after I had last spoken with Abby, I finally made contact. She had returned with three interns to continue her research. The amount of responsibility it took to organize and pull off the details of her complex study was impressive. She had begun in the late spring, working with government agencies, to collar wolves in our area. She then needed to hire a crew and arrange for their housing, as well as contact managers of nearby ranches for permission onto their property. Her public relations skills would be critical. Many locals mistrust government agencies and mistrust anything to do with wolves even more. And most crucial of all, she needed to be professional and non-biased in all her dealings. All opinions and research findings were strictly off-limits until her thesis was published. Neutrality was the key word.

The method of research was simple: several wolves were collared. The data was downloaded weekly. When an animal lingered in a certain location for longer than twenty minutes, that was an area of interest. Abby wanted to see what the wolves were eating and where they were moving. This information would hopefully be useful for management.

This was Abby's second, and final, year of field research before she'd head back to the university to analyze the data and write her thesis. Unfortunately, her luck wasn't so good this year with collaring. Three wolves had been collared. One male was traveling back and forth between the Park and the Absarokas to the east, and by mid-summer that wolf's collar registered a 'dead' signal. Most likely he'd been killed by wolves in the Park. One of the other collared wolves had been shot by Wildlife Services in response to some cattle predation. A familiar jargon heard was the '10J rule.' This was an agreement made when the initial introduction was drawn up. Essentially, it allowed for the federal government to have control to limit the amount of wolves in an area due to live-stock predation. That meant shooting wolves from the suspect pack by helicopters. Collaring wolves made finding the pack easier. And although it wouldn't be known which wolf or wolves killed a cow or sheep, reducing the pack size was the objective. And the wolves with collars were the easy targets. That left only one collared wolf Abby was following when I caught up to her that year. That wolf was a young female.

I told Abby that Koda had run after a wolf just weeks before.

"Koda and I were bushwacking around Little Sulphur Creek. Those meadows have a lot of dry arroyos. We were traveling along one that was lightly wooded and Koda was a little ahead of me. Suddenly he stopped, looked to the left, and before I could even figure out what was going on, Koda took off after a black wolf that had been quietly watching us in a gully about ten feet away. I was screaming for Koda to come back and thought I'd lost him. I was afraid there might be other wolves waiting to attack him. Finally, after a few minutes, he trotted back with a shit-eating grin on his face."

Abby told me that during the summer, the pack in my valley had gotten into trouble and killed a cow.

"Wildlife Services eliminated the entire pack except the alpha female and her yearling. You probably saw the yearling pup. Was she black, and small?"

The biggest wolf found in Yellowstone so far was 148 pounds, but normally a male will average about 100 pounds and a female around 85 pounds. I told Abby this wolf was small — smaller than ninety-pound Koda. Just the summer before, the valley had a pack of twelve wolves. Now, apparently, only these two were left.

I usually called Abby every week to see if she needed extra help locating 'areas of interest'. If we got there and it wasn't a kill site, we'd try and figure out what was going on. Was it a rendez-vous site? A lay? We'd note the GPS coordinates, but that was only accurate to within about a three-foot radius. So we needed to hunt around for clues like a confirmed wolf hair in a lay.

Abby taught me how to distinguish between an ungulate hair and a wolf hair. Our female wolf had been scrounging around the transfer station. This is a secondary service trash site for locals and bagged garbage only. It has several large dumpsters in a fenced, locked enclosure to keep bears out. A dirt road leads to the enclo-sure. But many people bring their dead animals and leave them outside the fenceline. In this case, a horse had been unloaded in the flats beyond the formal dumping area. Our wolf was hanging around here. There was definite evidence she'd chewed on some old bones. Abby had me look around for possible lay sites. I found evidence of one but couldn't tell if they were wolf. She called me over to one she'd identified. She bent down over a flattened grassy form. Most of the grass was dry. Deftly, she picked up a small hair, about 1/2" long. How in the world she saw that, I had no idea, for it was the same color as the tawny grass.

"Ungulates have hollow hair. The hairs break easily. Canine hairs are tough and usually short."

I told her that with my aging eyes, I'd need to probably get out my reading glasses to find that, or maybe use a bright spotlight.

She laughed. "You'll get it with time."

Sometimes Abby would let me bring Koda along. If she knew we weren't investigating a kill site, her dog would come too. After Koda's first expedition, he quickly figured out what we were doing. Pretty soon if we couldn't find the exact placement of a lay, confirmed by a hair, then Abby would call Koda over to employ his nose. For him, the work was natural. I joked that maybe I could start hiring him out.

Another day I went out to locate coordinates with Rebecca, one of the interns. We parked off the Beartooth highway and followed the coordinates through thick forest. Rebecca luckily had plugged our car coordinates into the GPS unit, because I was so turned around I'm not sure I'd have found my way out. We came to an area where she knew the wolf had hung around for several hours; she thought perhaps this small, enclosed meadow was used as a rendezvous site.

"In the summer, when the pups are bigger," Rebecca explained, "the adults take them to these safe sites where the pups can rest and play while the adults hunt. The funny thing is I've found 'toys' at these sites."

"Toys?" I was perplexed by that.

"Well, you know, people leave all sorts of things around when they're camping. Wolves are curious and will bring them back as playthings for their pups. Once I found a tennis ball, and another time I found a Sponge Bob toy."

Certainly this small clearing was full of flattened grass, fresh evidence of lays.

Rebecca told me that after an entire summer of following this wolf, she'd never seen any wolves while doing her research.

"Of course, the objective is to come in after the wolves are gone from the area. That's why we download the information from the collar a week later. If we think the wolves are still hanging around, then we won't go out till the following week. But I sure would like to see one up close and personal."

I accompanied either Abby or Rebecca or sometimes the whole crew many times over the course of that month. One morning I left earlier than usual to help the interns. We headed for a new location and parked on the dirt road below a large escarpment of burned timber. We scrambled through and over downed logs, eventually reaching the bottom of a series of large cliffs. The coordinates led us to several bedding sites.

Abby was inspecting what she thought was a bed site, but couldn't find any hairs.

"We need a dog sniff here" she called out.

I brought Koda over but he wasn't interested in her site. Instead, he began digging furiously by a log about six feet away. And sure enough, there's where we found a plethora of hairs. Koda had really begun to get the hang of his work here.

On the way back to their office, we stopped at the local store and restaurant. Besides the snacks and coffee required after hiking, the social time was just as important to the project as the field work. Abby made a beeline towards the bar area in the back and I soon followed. I found her on a stool, chatting with a fellow whom I'll call Jeff. I sat at a table with some of the locals.

Jeff's a talkative, red-faced, large man who seemed to revel in his story telling. I gathered he appreciated any shock value he could wring out of a story. Their conversation soon filled the room and everyone began listening to Jeff tell a tale about bobcats, about how he'd caught two of them in his homemade trap.

"Yeah," he said, "I came home and there was that bobcat in the tree next to my house. We got out my homemade trap, baited it with tuna fish. We caught both of them cats".

Big Pause here.

Finally, someone asked the question he was waiting for.

"What'd you do with them?"

Without a hint of hesitation, Jeff waved his arms with a lot of bravado, and then said, "Shot 'em in the head and sold 'em for $300 a piece."

Bragging about trapping and shooting bobcats, even for a good story, didn't sit well with me, especially when told with such meanness. On the way home I told Abby how I felt.

"The way he said that I could imagine him doing that to me."

She said he's one of the biggest wolf haters up here, but she and Jeff have made a truce.

"He's made it known to me that he thinks my study is a big waste of time and money 'cause there shouldn't be wolves here in the first place. And more than that, he's been interviewed several times as a suspect by Fish and Wildlife when a wolf has been illegally killed. But I've come to like Jeff regardless.

"Last summer there was this guy who had been bugging me for an interview. He said he was writing a book on the Environmental Protection Act and had just come from interviewing people in the park and wanted to interview me. I was really busy, up to my ears in trying to do my job here, but he just wouldn't quit. Finally I said to him, well, if you really want to talk to some locals and get an idea of what they think, go talk with Jeff. This man was from back East and I told him he'd probably find Jeff hanging around the store. By the time I got there, this guy was running out of the bar completely white-faced and he left in a hurry. I went in to talk with Jeff, he was red-faced and worked into a frenzy. I felt bad and apologized to him. You know, we'd become friends despite our differences. Somewhere along the line, we'd just agreed we could disagree."

After arriving at the ranger station, Abby showed me last year's GPS results plotted on several overlay maps. One map showed the movements over the summer of the resident elk herd on a nearby private ranch. The resident herd is in what is called the 'front country,' farther down the valley. The herd in our valley is a migratory herd, referred to as the 'back country herd'.

You could see little colored dots, one color representing the elk, and another color representing the collared wolves in that area. The elk were staying fairly high up, grazing along the forest/ meadow interfaces. If you put the two maps together, they overlaid almost perfectly — the wolves follow the elk. During most of the summer, no cattle depredations were found there, because the ranch's herd was grazing lower down in different pastures. But at the end of the summer the ranch put cattle in the area and, with the mix of wildlife and cattle, some predations occurred. And as soon as that happened, Wildlife Services were called in and they shot the wolves.

I suggested to her that her data might be used to note where the wolves follow deer and elk in the summer and therefore ranchers could keep cattle from those areas. This could work in forest service grazing areas because the range manager would tell the private ranchers each summer where their rotations are and the dates when to move their herds. Private ranchers would have to self-manage with this information.

When Abby's thesis report finally came out in 2011, that was exactly one of her recommendations for depredation control.

"...knowledge of ungulate distributions and migration patterns can help understand and predict hotspots of wolf conflict with livestock. Often the removal of depredating packs is a temporary solution..."

In addition, her thesis has several other suggestions for cattle management in wolf areas: awareness of den and rendezvous sites, as these can be hotspots for conflicts with cattle; avoid pasture rotations that bring cattle to higher elevations as the summer progresses, as this increases commingling with elk; and allow managed hunts on private lands in the fall to reduce commingling of elk and cattle.

As the season came to a close, the interns began peeling off, going back to school. Only a few remained till the end of October. This was the end of the study. I'd gotten to know quite a few of the girls on the crew and was sad the study was ending and they'd be gone. With the sale of my home that summer, my first winter here was approaching. Light snows had fallen, and the aspens and cottonwoods were already leafless. How would the valley feel with so few people here? Their youthful presence was happy company, and reminded me of my son, now far away at college in New York.

I returned late January from some remaining work in California, and was pleasantly surprised when Rebecca showed up to help with the winter elk study in the valley. As wolf movement patterns were important and necessary data for the elk study, Rebecca's main job that winter was to keep track of the comings and goings of a collared wolf who'd traveled to the area from Idaho. This female wolf's signal had been picked up by a local who helps with tracking wolves for the Park. It was a good sign for genetic exchange.

Rebecca took me out a few times looking for the female, nicknamed Spud. It was mating season and Spud seemed to be hanging out farther north around the easiest routes into and through the

Park almost every time we went out. Rebecca showed me how to use the telemetry antenna and how to chart the results on a map. Basically it was just like when I made landscape site plans by hand, except on a grand scale. For instance, if you want to locate a tree in your yard, you need to measure it from two points, Point A and Point B. A and B need to be points that are measured and marked from, say, your house corners. Then these points are triangulated and you have your tree location. The same principle applies to most accurate telemetry. We drove along the highway until we found a clear enough spot to receive a strong signal. First Rebecca located her position on the GPS. Then she held up the telemetry antenna and waved it around side to side till she found the direction of the strongest signal. This direction was noted with a compass reading. By using two or three locations, then plotting the points out on a map, you can get a general location of your animal.

Not long after, Rebecca and I got a signal on Spud down in the Clark's Fork canyon, below the dump where Abby and I had been in the summer. Although the dirt road to the dump didn't have much snow, Rebecca wanted to drive beyond it to try and see if she could visually see Spud. Not having seen a wolf during the summer study, she felt a special bond with Spud and was anxious for a sighting.

She drove the truck past the dump. Right away we got high-sided and totally stuck. After digging for an hour, scrounging around for wood in the dump or anything for traction, we finally got free — only Spud was long gone.

Eventually Rebecca's day came. Spud had on a collar that used a radio signal, but the U.S. Fish and Wildlife wanted a more high tech collar on Spud, one that could track her comings and goings by satellite. The agency helicopter was able to locate, dart and then re-collar her. To Rebecca's delight, she got to help put the new collar on the sedated wolf, stay with her till she awoke (a policy they had to prevent people from harming sedated wolves), plus ride back to the Cody airport in the helicopter.

* * * * * *

These had been stellar winter days, the sky blue and clear, the air dry and cold. Yesterday was Valentine's Day and we'd heard the wolves howling all day across the canyon. It's mating season for the wolves and they were actively vocal.

It was noon and Gary, who had come to help me burn piles of beetle-killed pines, was packing up to go back into Cody. Being a mountain boy at heart, having grown up in Montana, he'd been dawdling and getting a late start, resisting going back down to the high desert of the Big Horn Basin. His dog Sadie was with Koda outside and they'd begun barking up a ruckus. We looked out the front picture window and there, across the road a few hundred yards, was the pack. Five wolves running as fast as they could through the neighbors' meadows. Their herd of fifty horses paid them no mind and continued feeding as the wolves ran amongst them. Pulling up the rear and lagging way behind was a large grey male, limping. The pack high tailed across the road and up through the east meadows. We watched till they hit the divide and disappeared, all in the span of less than five minutes. A hike that takes over half an hour.

Gary went back to Cody and I back tracked the pack. They'd been making a loop between the valley, up over the high peaks and into the next drainage south. In the early morning, they'd made two kills — two older cow elks — right by the side of the main dirt road. A car driving by must have spooked the wolves off when we saw them running. They stayed on those kills, hanging around off and on for over a week. 'Limpy,' as I fondly named the big grey, mated with a young black wolf at the kill site mid-week.

By the following winter, between mange in the Park, and the first wolf hunting seasons in Montana and Idaho (Wyoming still didn't have an adequate plan for delisting), the northeast area outside the park had more healthy wolves than all of the Northern Range's. Three packs were continually fighting it out in the valley all winter, while another pack, the Beartooth Pack, stayed on the east side of the Clark's Fork. Wolf sightings were plentiful. Yet just one winter later, the local pack had mysteriously disappeared; their alpha female killed in the spring, full with pups, by another pack. Instead of almost forty wolves in four packs as in the previous year, there were just two local packs with a total of around fifteen wolves. Three wolves had been killed by Wildlife Services during the summer, but the low numbers seem mostly due to territorial fighting. It appeared that wolves self-manage through territorial competition, with their numbers fluctuating in response to available prey. In addition, elk cows now had over fifteen years of experience dealing with wolves after an absence of over one hundred years. Their ancient instincts were renewed. The resident pack was mostly killing deer, a much easier prey to take down and a sign of their inexperience.

Winter in the valley is a lonely time for humans. Hunting is over, and snowmobiling goes on further north where the snows are deeper. And although this is premier time for wolf viewing, I rarely see people from the nearby towns taking advantage of it. A local resident tells me about a lively contingent that meets daily for morning coffee and loves to complain about wolves. But, he says, if you ask those same people have you ever seen a wolf, or a track, or even heard one howl, the answer is usually no.

Not too long after I moved here, I encountered the local's opinion. It appeared they blamed wolves for everything. My friend Warren, a clergyman in Wyoming for over thirty-five years, summed up this scapegoat attitude eloquently. "It used to be the communists, then it was the coyotes, now it's the wolves. People always need someone to blame for their troubles."

I once talked with a woman whose parents ran an outfitting company. She was a teenager and already hated wolves. She told me a story about how one fall they had packed supplies up near the Yellowstone border in anticipation of bringing hunters up the next day to camp there. They'd left three dogs with the supplies, alone, overnight. This was something they were used to doing. Their family had been outfitting here for years before there were wolves. But this year was different. When they returned the following day, one of their dogs had been killed by wolves.

Mostly it's the hunting crowd who complains. Not all of them, but the ones who do are vocal. The story goes that the wolves are killing all the elk, reducing their numbers drastically. One biologist told me that many of the local outfitters moved here after the 1988 fires in Yellowstone. The fires created epic amounts of lush nutritious feed for the elk. Elk numbers spiked, which was partly why wolves were reintroduced. But twenty years later, those grasslands have turned into lodgepole pine forests, plus a ten year drought dried up other prime habitat. In many areas, elk numbers have returned to historical numbers (or carrying capacity), or dropped somewhat due to compromised habitat. What was the norm for the early 90s, isn't necessarily what is the norm for the Greater Yellowstone Ecosystem. And hunters and outfitters have a way of talking in memories and anecdotes rather than looking at the biology or the extended historical facts. Twenty or thirty years is their yardstick of comparison.

One early spring day soon after moving here I took a hike down the Lewis and Clark trail. It's an easy walk, hugging the nearby river before it begins its treacherous cascade down a thousand-foot chasm. There's a beautiful little waterfall, hidden off-trail that was my destination.

I noticed a lot of moose sign in the willows around the river — fresh droppings and prints were everywhere. A pair of nesting ospreys watched from a dead snag. I sat and enjoyed watching these fish hawks for a while. The female was sitting on her nest, although she took some time out to try and scare me off. The male sat nearby with a piece of fish in his talons.

After lunch, bushwacking back to the trail, I ran into a fellow resting his horse. I introduced myself.

"Find any horns?" he asked.

People around here spend lots of time looking for horns, or antlers, shed in the spring. They could be worth big money or simply provide an excuse to hike or ride in the backcountry.

"Nope, wasn't looking for any," I replied. "But I did find a pair of nesting ospreys and moose sign."

"I saw four wolves up on table mountain. They'll eat your dog, you know. Just like that."

"Yep, that's why I keep him on that electronic collar. We have an agreement he and I. I protect him from wolves and he watches for bears."

"Those frickin' wolves, they've ruined everything. There used to be so many bull elk here. I wish they'd never put them here. There're some denning up there on the mountain. They're everywhere. They ran after an elk right through the trailer park the other day."

I mentioned that I liked having them in the landscape, but he wasn't listening to what I thought.

"There's no more moose anymore. They're history. The wolves've frickin' ruined it all. Things used to be good."

It's unclear whether moose are even native to these areas of Wyoming. Osborne Russell never mentioned moose once in his diary. In all my readings of the indigenous peoples here, I haven't run across anything about moose bones or antlers used as tools or found in their middens. Sporadic observations of moose appeared in northwest Wyoming after 1850, but it's believed the population didn't begin to increase and expand until after the establishment of Yellowstone Park. In addition, studies have shown that the 1988 fires devastated habitat for moose. Moose suffer heat stress in winter when temperatures are above 23 degrees F, and in summer above 57 degrees. Above 80 degrees for extended periods, without adequate refuge, is unsuitable. Moose need coniferous forests for refuge during the day, and for forage in winter. The extensive '88 fires habitat loss, as well as increasing beetle-kill, climate change, and disease may account for the majority of our moose population declines.

The fellow continued, clearly uninterested in my assessment. "Last year we found three bull elk kills up Crandall creek. Those wolves just hone in and kill them. They're killers you know. They kill just for sport sometimes."

I mentioned all the grizzlies in the area.

"Oh, those grizzlies don't do much. It's those damn wolves."

These are people who live on the land and know the land, at least in a certain way. They feel comfortable seeing grizzlies, but not wolves. And they resent having to take them into account now. They know where the wolves den even though the U.S. Fish and Wildlife Service keep it secret.

The wolf reintroduction was a massive undertaking requiring over ten years of hard work. There were many people who put their reputations on the line in order to bring the wolf back into a landscape when, just seventy years before, the campaign was complete eradication of the animal. A lot of fanagling and political wrangling had to go on behind the scenes to push the reintroduction through. When the political green light came, then all the logistics of trapping Canadian wolves, transporting them, and holding them in the pens had to be considered. As to public opinion, Renee Askins writes in *Shadow Mountain,*

"Beginning in April 1992, there were thirty-four open houses held in the three regional states, and seven in other parts of the country, to identify what issues people wanted to be considered in the EIS (Environmental Impact Statement). More than 1,730 people attended these meetings and nearly 4,000 comments were received. In the next phase...twenty-seven open houses and seven formal hearings were held in the three regional states and three national locations. Nearly 2,000 people attended the meetings and about 5,000 comments were received. In the final phase of the process, stretching from July 1, 1993, to November 26, 1993, twelve formal hearings were held throughout the country. Never had there been such an extensive effort to poll public opinion on a wildlife issue. The results overwhelmingly favored wolf restoration...A record-breaking 160,000 comments were received on the EIS alone, the most on any EIS in history, and in the final count they favored the return of wolves by a two-to-one margin."

The effort just to bring the wolf back was so massive, with so many roadblocks, that key education of the public was put on the back burner. One environmentalist told me,

"How are the local public supposed to feel? I mean, the government spent millions of dollars and lots of years exterminating wolves. Now they're bringing them back! To people who've lived here for generations, this makes no sense. The big mistake they made was not enough education on why they planned the reintroduction campaign."

Most people who hate wolves don't look squarely at the biology involved or the improved habitat health that the wolves bring. They're either ranchers, making a living off livestock that wolves consume, or they're hunters who think "less predators, more prey." Education regarding why we need carnivores in the landscape is an issue that will be ongoing for many years. Much of the recent science regarding carnivores and healthy ecosystems is still trickling down into state wildlife management.

The intense emotion and hatred felt towards wolves isn't really about wolves at all. Ed Bangs, the wolf recovery coordinator for U.S. Fish and Wildlife puts it this way:

"You have to remember wolves and wolf management has nothing to do with reality. I mean we can give you facts, you know, all the biology stuff. That isn't what people talk about. They're talking about what wolves mean to them symbolically."

Those symbolic implications date back to 1300 Europe. Forest habitat was being burned for rangelands and farming and wolves were beginning to turn to sheep and cattle for food. But the European hatred towards wolves really began with the Black Death. Peaking in Europe in the mid-14th century, more than one third of the population succumbed to the disease. The Black Death was terrifying as well as efficient. People who went to bed perfectly healthy could be dead by morning. Whole villages died in a few weeks. Doctors refused to see patients, priests wouldn't administer last rites, families left their spouses and children to die. The sheer volume of dead bodies meant graves were not practical. Instead, bodies were left in place, piled outside the towns or dumped into rivers. Wolves, along with cats and dogs, were spotted feeding on the carcasses. Wolves became a symbol of all that was untamed and unpredictable, a symbol of evil and death. After the plague, bounties were placed on wolves as their habitat diminished further. When Europeans came to the Americas, they brought with them their attitudes towards wilderness and wildlife. These things had to be dominated and controlled before the New World would be safe for settlement.

Yet Native Americans had successfully lived with wolves for thousands of years. Observing how wolves moved through the landscape, many tribes looked to them as a role model for their scouts who needed to detect danger from warring bands. Sometimes scouts themselves were even called 'wolves'. Highly territorial, wolves can detect through scent and marking where other packs' boundaries are. They are constantly probing, making extra-territorial forays, singularly or in groups. And not surprisingly, it doesn't take them long, a few weeks or even days, to pick up on vacancies.

Jon Young, a professional tracker, describes wolves in this way:

"They move with such stealth and perfection that their tracks are like poetry of perfection. Even traveling at high speeds, they place their tracks in such a proper manner. They are masters of energy conservation even while moving."

He goes on to say that wolves need to cover great distances to find food, sometimes over thirty miles in one night. All the while they are practicing invisibility. This is a quality that scouts looked to emulate. Scouts had to run long distances in silence, use their peripheral vision even at night, then bring all that information back to the tribe. Wolves, like these native scouts, traveled at the edge of night. Wolves are masters of illusions, staying at the edges.

"They are the ultimate power in awareness. Keen eyesight, very intelligent, heightened sense of hearing, and an amazing sense of smell — all their senses combine to create enormous instinctive ability," says Young.

* * * * * *

It is the spring of 2012 and I am attending a public information meeting in Cody. The Wyoming Game & Fish is about to present an overview of Wyoming's first wolf hunt next October. In most of Wyoming, the speaker says, wolves will be labeled as 'predator status,' meaning they can be shot on sight. A large map is on the wall. It shows a tiny portion of the state, the northwestern areas around Yellowstone National Park, where wolves will be labeled 'trophy game' with a hunt season. The rest of the state, over 80%, wolves will be fair game anytime, anywhere, by any means.

"Our first hunt will be conservative," the speaker continues. "We have to maintain ten breeding pairs and one hundred wolves in order for them not to be relisted as endangered."

I see the hunt in my area will have a limit of eight wolves. Yet I know that before this spring's denning season we barely had twelve wolves in the two packs. The pack in my valley usually gets into some trouble killing a few calves, and our elk herd numbers are down. By dividing the Trophy Management Areas into smaller units, the Wyoming Game and Fish felt they'd have greater control to target wolves for livestock damage or elk predation issues. So I wasn't surprised, then, to see the attempt to greatly reduce the wolves in this area. A wolf license will cost around $18 and I am already envisioning the rush of hunters, from October through December, fired up with a meanness of spirit to 'pop' a wolf. I wonder how many years it will take until they've accumulated sufficient trophies on their walls to cool their hatred down. People don't eat wolf.

Renee Askins notes, "The first wave of wolf killing took place in the 1870s. Records indicate a take of 100,000 wolves a year between 1870 and 1877 in the state of Montana alone." It doesn't take much to do the math to envision the historical population.

Today over 1700 wolves live in the three Rocky Mountain recovery states of Idaho, Montana, and Wyoming. The delisting plans set by U.S. Fish and Wildlife calls for a minimum of one hundred wolves in Wyoming, and 150 in Montana and in Idaho. If the count falls below, the wolf will be relisted. Certainly there is not the same amount of plentiful game as in the 1870s; and we live in an era where land has been partitioned off for residences, farms and ranches. But four hundred wolves in that large of an area would not insure enough genetic diversity to support a healthy population of wolves.

* * * * * *

Throughout the winter before delisting I had seen the alpha female and her yearling hunting together. In the spring my friend Don and his brother had been antler hunting when they inadvertently ran into her den.

"There's four pups there." They told me excitedly.

We went back the following day to put up a trail camera, but Don's accidental presence seemed to have caused the adults to move their pups elsewhere. Not wanting to stick around the den site much longer in case the wolves or pups returned, I hiked up an adjacent canyon only to discover a cougar den. The den was high up the canyons' walls. I side plained around the coulee, circling its perimeter, then clambered downhill via a narrow streambed to follow the cat's tracks. A thin deer trail on the ravine's edge helped me negotiate a large boulder blocking the streambed. When I looked up, I spied a yearling wolf watching me from behind a tree about twenty feet ahead. I stopped and we studied each other for a brief moment, then she ran off and joined her mom in the nearby meadows. I hurried round a bend in the trail to view her mother, the black alpha female. She'd been moving her pups to a new secure site. She paused, considered me, then ran off. I find wolves are

They inadvertently ran into her den.

ever curious about the comings and goings of humans. These two wolves who'd I'd seen many times over the course of the year will probably not last to see another winter. I knew that. They were too used to human presence.

Because I feel wolves belong in the landscape, I get accused of 'being on the side' of the wolf. Yet there are no sides here, though someone must speak for wolf. And what would that person say? He might say wolves are elegantly fitted to be apex predators. We need the wolves, he would say. Their job is to herd the elk. Wolves shepherd the elk so they don't over browse the young trees and shrubs and denude our bottomlands. He might tell us that wolves will control coyotes and in doing so antelope babies will thrive. Maybe he'd tell us his hopes and dreams: about our lynx returning in greater numbers because with less coyotes there will be

...only to discover a cougar den

more snowshoe hares, the primary lynx food. And he'll dream the beavers will return in greater numbers because with less browsing around the creeks, they will have more trees and shrubs with which to build their dams; and when our beavers return, our fish will have cool deep waters to hide in with more detritus and bugs to eat.

And possibly this person would choose to speak for wolf in a poetic manner. He'd talk about conscious choices we humans can make concerning wildness and wildlife; how we can trace, through our feelings and actions, natural cycles, rhythms as old as mountains, and build a new ethical foundation upon which to live and make choices. He'd remind us how we have walked on this road, with these animals, for a long time; and truly they have walked the road longer than we have, carrying secrets we have yet to learn. And that is why we need them all, the complete reservoir of wildlife; they are worlds unto themselves that we have yet to touch.

With that sensitivity, we treat all things around us, living and non-, with a sacredness, a thankfulness, and an acceptance that is most true to our human nature. With reverence as our guide, we can allow wolves to be wolves, doing what they're best fitted to do, and have been doing for thousands of years in their dance with elk and deer and bison.

We are afraid of life, which is a strange thing to say considering how hard we try and hang on to it. We are constantly suppressing it, attempting to harness and control those forces, creating little niches where we feel safe and comfortable. This is why it is easier for us to destroy, tear things apart, sully our environment, and create the illusion of predictability, than to embrace Life in all its wild and wooliness. To be in life implies being overwhelmed, swept away, carried like a raft in a great ocean, humbled, acknowledging our smallness and our connectedness.

One spring evening at dusk, driving home from Cody, three wolves ran across the road in front of my car. Beginning their night's hunt, their *joie de vivre* was the very embodiment of the immense, wondrous, yet terrifying Power that is the Universe itself. Wolves, in their ceaseless energy, their deep intelligence, epitomize the purity and dynamism of Life. Maybe that is why humans have spent so much time and effort trying to control and eliminate them. They are the *emblem* of true, unabashed, Freedom.

joie de vivre

The force that through the green fuse drives the flower
Drives my green age; that blasts the roots of trees
Is my destroyer. And I am dumb to tell the crooked rose
My youth is bent by the same wintry fever.

Dylan Thomas

CHAPTER 5

A Most Magnificent Animal

There's always something special about seeing an elk, whether one or more than a hundred. They are a magnificent animal, sleek and beautiful. Although they are cervids, like deer and moose, to me they move differently, their look is more ancient. In their winter coats, they are regal. In summer, their luscious reddish-brown fur shines and calls to be touched. Yet unlike deer, they have a heightened skittishness. More of a herd animal than deer, they depend on one another. A deer will prick up its ears and listen. An elk senses the air and the emotion of the herd for danger. The elk will even watch the deer amongst them for a sign of danger. Sometimes, when I see a large group prancing this way and that in the bitter chill of winter, they appear almost camel-like. It is one of the great wonders of temperate North America to still have large herds of these animals to overpower man's senses and instill wonder. I never tire of watching them.

Early on I'd heard how the Yellowstone Park elk congregate in the winters in the valley, but I was never here at the right time of year. A few years after purchasing my home, I came in early spring for a few weeks with hopes of seeing them. My neighbor, Jack, had told me, "Just drive up the road before dusk and you'll see the elk."

So one evening late in April, I took the beat-up '78 Dodge that came with the house and drove up to the wind swept clearing above. I was surprised to see Jack's truck sitting on the roadside. He'd come up alone, parked by the side of the road and was watching a large herd of about three hundred elk; he had an old scope and an antique heavy pair of binoculars.

"They're magnificent animals," he tells me.

I jumped in his truck and we sat on this lonely wintery dirt road, watching these elk do what they've been doing for thousands of winters — feeding, moving silently and gracefully. Dusk came in like a blanket upon us, while a light snow whipped the landscape. I felt as if I was reliving an ancestral ritual, tied together in a strange familiar bond with this old man next to me. We could have just as easily been behind a rock instead of in the warmth of his pick-up

Jack's a dying breed of men; his birthday was soon and he was turning eighty-four. He grew up on his family homestead in the valley. He is closer at heart to an American bushman than to the modern-day hunters who watch these elk during the fall hunting season.

"I never tire of watching game," he told me. "One time I watched a bull elk breed a cow; and a bull moose mount a mule. Of course, they can't really breed, but they tried."

"Sometimes," he tells me, "I sit for hours and watch them from the window of my trailer."

I loved that he was out there watching elk, even after year upon year of watching them. I loved that there were more elk in this valley than people who live here. I loved that today I saw more animals than people — two people to the hundreds of elk.

When the tables are turned, when the populations are upside-down to what we've been accustomed to, we remember our place on the land, and the Earth. There is a naturalness to it. We relax and our awareness opens.

* * * * * *

In the winter of 2009-2010 we had near record snows, in some areas 300-600% above average. The late snow melt at the higher elevations landlocked the Yellowstone Lamar migratory elk herd in the valley till early June. Usually by late April most have headed back to the park to have their babies. But this year, with the heavy snow pack in the high country, more elk were giving birth at lower elevations.

On the 31st of May I spied a lone elk crossing in and out of the willow patches below my house. These willows abut the nearby forest on one side and the county road on the other. Across the road lies a large expanse of irrigated horse pasture. I watched the cow for a few days. It appeared she'd feed for a time with a larger group of elk grazing in the meadows then disappear into the willows. Over the course of days she appeared more and more concerned and agitated. I had a feeling there was a calf hidden in the brush, which she was nursing.

A few days later, from my window, I observed her making her way over to the bushes as usual, but this time she was accompanied by a cadre of seven cow elk. It was around dusk and I watched the elk walk in line into the willows and disappear among the undergrowth. I knew the paths the elk take in and out of the forested areas and this was not one of them. To see a group following the lone cow was definitely odd.

The following day I took my bear spray and cautiously went to investigate. I followed an animal path into the thickets while the elk were occupied feeding across the way. In a muddy area of the creek, now widened by slash and blow downs from last year's logging, was a large and unmistakable grizzly print. The print was fresh and moving towards a small clearing ahead. Tracking the print, I found the calf, completely consumed. Only the skin and legs remained. I could see the mother elk had tried to hide her baby well. The remains of its tiny body lay in a heap in tall grass, protected by a freshly fallen spruce bough. I inspected the little legs and skin. The calf had deftly and perfectly been skinned.

Six out of ten elk calves are predated upon within the first ten days of their lives. They are fairly helpless for those first two weeks. Many people say the calves don't have a scent, but I would disagree. I don't usually see bear tracks in these marshy areas, yet it

Only the skin and legs remained.

was obvious from the tracks that this grizzly had made a beeline to that calf. He hadn't wandered through the woods inspecting different areas. He knew exactly where to go for this meal.

I picked up the calf's skin and brought it up to my nose. It still had a sweet, young smell, like a puppy's or a baby's, a kind of freshness not common on carcasses. The odor wasn't strong, and staying low to the ground kept the calf's scent down, but to a grizzly, I was sure it was pretty potent.

I wondered: Why, last night, did I see seven cow elk accompany mama elk into the willows? Was that a show of sympathy and support?

The following morning my lone mother elk wandered the forest and marsh, calling for hours for her calf. At one point she stood on the rise behind my house, bugling a mournful song. I went outside and watched her. I felt tremendous sadness. I knew she didn't know what happened to her calf, just that it was gone.

A line from Pema Chodron, a Buddhist teacher, came into my thoughts: "…that feeling in your stomach of 'I don't want this to be happening.' You try to escape it in some way, but if somehow you could stay present and touch the rawness of the experience, you can really learn something."

So although her lament pained me in deep and familiar ways, I thought it important to stay with her and listen. It was a simple company I could keep, no different than a human might offer comfort by listening and sitting with another in a time of grief. Her bugles were low, guttural — neither the bull elk's high-pitched sounds you hear in the fall nor the cow elk's sounds you hear in the spring when she calls to her calf if she senses danger. These cries came from a deep, primeval place, not unlike the wails of humans mourning.

After a time the cow left the high ridge above my home, hoping to find her calf across the sagebrush flats. That would be the last I'd see of her. The day was young with a hint of the approach of summer. This experience of deep universal loss still with me, I thought I'd hike to a favorite spot — a high prominence that overlooks a wide canyon — and have lunch there. A quiet kind of meditation perhaps. The hike climbed to the top of a sandstone rim through a patchwork of forests and meadows. Once on the plateau above, I could see a large meadow feed into a triangular wedged-shaped cliff with the river hundreds of feet below. It's a striking view and a solitary place.

As soon as I broke through the trees into the summit's meadow, I spied a solitary elk. She seemed a bit nervous at my presence (not unusual) but then I saw something else. A calf lay nearby. A wet calf. She had just given birth and probably just finished licking the calf clean of the afterbirth. I made a large circle and hid behind some rocks out of the wind near the cliff's edge.

Mom took off and left her baby there, a common strategy, hoping she could lure me away from her newborn. I watched the newborn for over an hour. Within the first ten minutes, he tried to stand up. He struggled unsuccessfully on his weak legs. Exhausted, he then spent another ten minutes resting. But soon he tried again. This time, although it still wasn't easy, he was getting stronger. He'd rest for a while, then try again. During that entire hour, his mother never returned. In the course of one day, I'd witnessed death and birth — the sight of this newborn wet calf a salve to my spirits.

His mom seemed to have chosen a well-protected place for her calf's first few weeks of life. High up, the only easy entrance to the meadows was the side from which I'd arrived. The calf lay next to a rock with similar coloring. All this gave me a good feeling about his survival. If this little calf made it through a few more days, he'd be too fast for bears. And if he made it through a month or so, when the snows melt, his mom will take him up to the Absaroka Divide to spend his first summer. He'd have a good year this year, more similar to what his ancestors used to experience before the long ten-year drought, because the grasses would stay greener for longer.

Then next January I might see him again when he migrates back down here for the winter. He'll be taller but still a youngster and still vulnerable to the wolves and the deep winter snows. But he might just be one of the tougher ones, the lucky ones, and live into his adulthood, live to mate — and not be caught by a hunter's bullet.

One month later I hiked with some friends up to the same prominence. I wanted to see if there was any sign that this calf had

Young elk calf

been predated upon. I searched the entire area and found no evidence; I could only hope that the calf had found its legs and was off to the higher peaks with its mother for a summer of good fresh grass.

* * * * * *

The carrying capacity of the valley in winter, I've been told, is about 1500 head of elk. Since that first spring I've seen over seven hundred elk grazing in January on the meadows where the divide separates the valley snows between deep and wind-blown. Another herd of similar size congregates in high pastures further down the valley at the Wilderness boundary.

Sometime around late February, early March, these herd sizes diminish and it's more usual to see smaller groups, around fifty to one hundred, sometimes less. The herds begin to move into other areas, usually farther east, taking advantage of new grazing areas that become exposed and clear of snow. Why they start out in these large herds, and slowly break up as winter wanes has been a mystery. Possibly the deeper snows early in the season make for harder travel. A larger herd would provide for greater safety with the restricted movement. As the elk become restless to give birth and head back to the high country, the diminishing snow allows them to flee danger faster. Maybe they are separating into smaller family groups as well.

As the herd sizes tighten, getting smaller by April, they are less and less visible till one day, they're all gone. By the time summer rolls around and the valley is crowded with more people than elk, I realize I'm missing them.

Because our elk travel to the high ridges of the Park, it's rare to see even one elk in the summer. Many people who've lived here since the 70s say there used to be a lot more resident year-round elk. But Jack tells me while he was growing up, in the 30s and 40s, there were few elk at all, winter or summer. It wasn't until sometime around the early 60s, he recalls, that the large herd changed their migration patterns and came to the valley in the winter. We still have resident elk and on rare occasions I've caught an elk on my trail camera during the summer. So when a friend and I took a ridgeline hike one mid-summer, we had no expectations of seeing elk. This ridge continues far west, eventually circling south to merge with the ridges of the deep backcountry, far from any roads. It's a steep ascent up the saddle, but once you're on the spine of the mountain, it's one continuous glorious meadow as far as the eye can see, broken only by stubby nubs of rock. The entire valley where I live was once a glacial lake, the surrounding cliffs of limestone from ancient seas. The limestone was buried by volcanics fifty million years ago. Eroded igneous rock exposes hints of these sediment layers underneath. All makes for present-day breathtaking views.

We rounded a rocky bend and lying in the high altitude summer sun were eight cow elk as if they were sunbathing. We watched for a while. They were sunbathing! During the cold winter months, I'm used to seeing elk hiding in the trees during the day using it as cover from wolves. They tend to come out to the open areas at dawn and dusk to feed. If there's a storm coming, or it's really cold, they'll feed earlier in the day. Yet here, in the high meadows at mid-summer, was this small, relaxed family group, taking their time to soak up the sun and digest their food. Earlier on the ridge we had spooked five bulls into a small woods. These you could call resident elk. If I can walk it in a day, they're not very far away.

* * * * * *

Abby told me that Arthur Middleton, a PhD candidate, was looking for a place to house his interns for a winter of fieldwork. Arthur was coordinating his second season of a three-year elk study with the purpose of understanding why this migratory herd had low cow/calf ratios. The study, paid for by various agencies, private and public, wanted to know why. Wolves were the prime suspects. His research would hopefully give some good scientific data and explanations.

The winter of 2008-2009 was to be my first winter in Wyoming since completing winterizing the cabin. I'd sold my home in California that summer, but I still had some jobs in the Bay Area. As I'd be working in California till late January, Arthur and I arranged for his crew to stay in my cabin January through early February. I called him late December to go over the details of his use of the cabin.

"Sorry it's taken me so long to get back to you," Arthur answered. "I've had a bad few days. I'm trying to get some wolves collared and I have to coordinate the helicopter and plane use with federal and state agencies. Everything was worked out, then Dead Indian Pass clocked 120 mph winds and we had to cancel. Now I have to reschedule it all over again and hope for better weather."

I told him how to open up the cabin, turn the water on, and other basics.

"We did everything right. I don't know what happened." It was January 5th; Arthur was on the phone.

"I made sure to warm up the cabin before I turned on the water; but when I opened the valve into the cabin, water started pouring out everywhere from the wall in the front bathroom."

Apparently an old PVC pipe had cracked directly in the wall. In the dead of winter, from my perch in California, somehow I had to find a plumber willing to travel over the pass and fix my plumbing. Plus lay in the crawl space in below-zero weather. While the interns stayed in town, I luckily did find a willing plumber and, in three days, he re-plumbed the entire house. Once the plumbing was done, the interns moved in for the month.

Arthurs' interns, dedicated kids all of twenty-three years old, rose every morning at 6 a.m., no matter how freezing it was, bundled up, and went out with their scopes to watch elk for several hours. They were gathering data to help understand why this backcountry herd is in trouble. Another team, stationed in the front country, mirrored the protocol. The difference was the front country herd was a resident herd and had normal cow/calf ratios. The comparison of the two herds, resident to migratory, would be a key factor in analyzing the final data. The task of the interns was to watch a collared elk for fifteen minutes and write down what that particular elk was doing. They used hand recorders in the field. "Elk number 27 standing, now sitting, now feeding"; they wiled away their days by counting the elk in the herds. Over time they could easily discern a yearling from a two year old. They told me that they'd seen elk chewing on another elk's antlers.

I was curious about the deer and elk and how much their diets overlapped. I saw them grazing together a lot.

In biology there's a fancy term called 'resource partitioning,' which basically means that deer and elk just couldn't be competing for the same foods in the same area or there wouldn't be enough food. Apparently big sagebrush (*Artemisia tridentata*) is an important food in the winter. The guys think the elk eat the sage when the snow cover is high because it's taller than the grass. As the new grasses emerge, the elk migrate elevationally, eating the new growth. The sage, though, provides protein that the grasses don't. According to studies, grasses comprise 75% of an elks' diet, whereas only about 25% of a mule deers. Elk are grazers, deer are browsers. The guys told me that the elk get first choice from their observations.

By late January, Rebecca had returned to join the interns and work on a separate aspect of Arthur's project. She would stay with me while the guys had gone over to the Game and Fish cabins. One early morning she and I went out to join the rest of the crew to watch the elk being darted. Ninety-two collared elk in the herd were captured at two critical times of the year – in late summer, after the annual period of fat gain, and in late winter, after the period of fat loss. Elk nutrition specialists were flown out from Washington state just for this part of the study. The collared elk were located by plane, then darted from helicopter to measure body fat, take blood and measurements, then given an ultrasound, all in five minutes. Dangerous work, copter pilots from a New Zealand company were hired. These pilots were used to maneuvering in the steep mountainous terrain of New Zealand to dart sheep. The copters would hone in on the desired elk, flying as low as possible for the darting. The scientists then jumped out, did their work on the temporarily sleeping elk, and within minutes the elk was on its feet and off running again. Unfortunately, in driving the elk like this in winter, a few elk always die from the stress.

From the ground, as these things usually go, there was a lot of standing around waiting. Mid morning we watched the helicopter spend over half hour trying to push a large group of elk outside the Wilderness boundary. No darting is allowed in Wilderness areas.

The herd of over five hundred elk moved like a flock of birds on the hillside, waves streaming back and forth, flowing in one direction then suddenly reversing and moving in another. Beautiful wave upon wave of elk, running in synchrony — lovely to watch but deadly tiring for the elk, already stressed nutritionally in late winter.

One helicopter maneuver I watched in amazement. On a very steep, rocky hillside, the desired elk was darted. How, I wondered, was the copter going to land? The hillside was more than a sixty-degree slope. The solution: it didn't land. Instead, it hovered five feet above the ground, the scientists jumped out, did their business as I watched the copter swinging back and forth off the windy slope, making a few passes so the strong winds didn't whip the machine into the hillside, then circle back around just high enough so they could hop back into the copter.

Dangerous work — darting elk.

The most interesting findings of Arthur's study was that the migratory elk were breeding every other year. Only an average of 68% of the cows were pregnant compared to a usual rate of around 90% for Rocky Mountain elk. This herd had only fifteen calves surviving per one hundred cows. A good average would be three times that many. With so many fingers pointed at wolves, the results and conclusions would be important for the fate of these predators.

In April I had a good-bye party at my cabin for the elk crew and friends. It was cold and snowing hard. By 5 p.m. everyone was having a good time, eating, telling stories except for Arthur who was conspicuously absent. Arthur had told the interns he needed one last piece of data before finishing up the season. He was hiking up difficult snowy terrain twenty minutes north of here. He'd been receiving a lot of telemetry signals from his collared wolves in this particular steep ravine and he wanted to know why they spent so much time up there. He'd said he'd be a little late and to start without him.

The talk turned to anecdotes of winter escapades of the locals and interns. The ranch hand from down the road entertained us with his fishing tales. He'd gone fishing under the old bridge and there was a grizzly, already about this early in the year. One of the interns stationed in the desert front country regaled us with stories of male sage grouse in leks performing their strutting displays for the females.

At 7:30 it was still snowing fiercely with no sign of Arthur. The guys joked that they'd look for him in the morning. But the truth was, they couldn't have gone out in this storm. Around 8:30 p.m. a bedraggled, wet, and hungry Arthur showed up. We let him get warm and well-fed, then asked what he'd seen up there. Arthur said he had hiked six miles up the north river trail in deep snow.

"There were several fairly fresh kills along the way. At one of them was a grizzly I spooked off the kill. At another there were wolves hanging around in the forest above the kill. Both the kills were big bulls, and when I went to check on their health by looking at their marrow, they were in bad shape. On the way back, in the dark, I kept looking for a place to spend the night. I didn't think I'd be able to make it back."

We locals were hungry for Arthur's thoughts so far on the study. You could see he already had a lot of data, and was trying to piece it together, like parts of a puzzle. He was thoughtful and non-prejudiced, working hard on the question of why this herd is in such poor shape with so few calves. I admired Arthur. He was dedicated almost to the point of craziness to get his information in order to decipher what was going on.

In all their modeling, no differences were found in elk habitat use or foraging due to predators.

Several years later, Arthur defended his dissertation, which I watched live online. When all the data was analyzed, the study debunked the idea that wolves cause indirect non-consumptive behavioral changes in elk, such as higher vigilance, increased stress, reduced feeding, lower body fat, or lowered pregnancy rates. In all their modeling, no differences were found in habitat use or foraging due to predators. Predation risk was definitely not a factor here. The fat these animals gained during the summer growing season was the key determinant of where they ended up in late winter. In fact, in many cases, the troubled migratory herd was actually fatter than the resident herd in March.

So what was going on here? Arthur evaluated green up patterns over a twenty-year period in the high country where migrants traveled each spring through fall. The 'green up period' is when elk readily regain fat lost over the winter; fat critical for nursing, breeding, becoming pregnant next fall and making it through the following winter. For this Yellowstone migratory herd, fattening up occurs in the high-elevation areas. What he found from looking at historical climate records was that the green-up period was becoming more and more compressed. This was due to higher temperatures in spring and summer as well as less spring precipitation and snow pack. Over the past twenty years the Yellowstone area has experienced an increase in July temperatures of eight degrees Fahrenheit. To observe these patterns, one has to take the long view over many years, not just year to year. These elk were suffering from poor nutrition during a critical time when they were about to give birth, begin lactation, and store new fats for another pregnancy in the fall.

Another factor affecting this herd was increased calf predation from grizzly bears. I'd observed this first hand, seeing elk calves taken by bears two years in a row that had birthed by my cabin. Grizzly bears have increased in the last decades with protection. Simultaneous with their increased numbers has been a decrease in their key forage foods such as white bark pine nuts. In addition, milder winters due to climate changes make for less winter-killed ungulates; also a major food source for spring-emerging bears.

From all of Arthur's research, it was apparent to him that the long historical relationship between wolves and elk fully equipped elk to contend with these predators. In the span of things, the seventy years that wolves have been absent from this landscape has not changed the evolutionary hard wiring in elk.

Instead of managing for wolves and elk in the landscape, the implications of this study suggest we should be looking at managing for whole and healthy ecosystems. With migrant animals, we need to consider their entire range, winter and summer, as opposed to manipulating predator-prey ratios.

There are many parts in the puzzle of healthy habitat and wildlife preservation: connectivity, sprawl management, public lands ranching, reestablishment of top predators, elk feeding grounds and disease, oil and gas interests, climate change mitigation, the list goes on. In appeasing this or that special interest or this or that part, we lose sight of the whole.

The Buddha tells a parable. A King has a group of blind men brought to the Palace and asks each of them to describe an elephant. When each blind man has touched a part of the elephant, the king asks them one by one: 'Well, blind man, have you seen the elephant? Tell me, what sort of thing is an elephant?" Each blind man describes the elephant differently. The first one who touched the elephant's ear says he is like a fan. The next who touched his leg and says he is like a tree trunk. The man who felt his tusk says he is like a spear. Another exclaims the elephant is like a wall. The last who touched his trunk says he is like a rope.

We, too, are all like the blind men for we cannot see the whole and all the parts are too many, too intricate, and some parts are even invisible. Yet left alone, the Whole can self-manage and heal itself quite well, without our interference.

The question is not how do we humans manage and juggle everything. The question is how can we live lightly, in right relationship to all around us? How do we utilize resources in the most effective and efficient manner possible, mitigating habitat loss that results from sprawl and greed? Can we concentrate our communities in such a way as to maximize wild spaces? How can our communities become self-sufficient, minimizing the need for new roads and high volume traffic that cuts through habitat? It is a puzzle of questions, but we must think differently if we are to preserve large tracts of healthy landscapes. By coming together to plan our communities with wildlife in mind, we will have space for large herbivores and the top predators that make for healthy habitat. This is what will guide us in this new century, towards a philosophy of the Whole.

"I am interested in the way that a man looks at a given landscape and takes possession of it in his blood and brain...None of us lives apart from the land entirely; such an isolation is unimaginable...We Americans need now more than ever before — and indeed more than we know — to imagine who and what we are with respect to the earth and sky. I am talking about an act of the imagination, essentially, and the concept of an American land ethic."

N. Scott Momaday

CHAPTER 6

Woods, Water, and Wildlife

I may be the only human to walk through the forest by my cabin on a regular basis. The woods mark a denseness, like a mohawk hairdo, between the meadow where my home sits and the meadows that flow up the large southwestern drainage. It's a compact forest with a graduated uphill slope that ends against a buttress of limestone. A series of rimrock stair steps higher and higher until you can go no further. The cliff top above has no real name, but local folklore calls it Mt. Herman, after Herman Ellsbury, the man who owned a sawmill and built my house in 1957. Douglas fir and limber pines intersperse their way up the summit. An ecotone exists where I walk the path through the forest. In those five minutes you cross over seven springs. These springs emerge from the limestone year round, never freezing; pure snow melt that seeps deep into fissures off the mountains' limestone structure. My water source is one of these springs.

My water has been a source of fascination since I arrived. Shortly after closing escrow, I received a call in early April from Dave, the contractor who had helped me with the final inspections. He was putting in a door to the crawl space and for some reason decided to check the levels in the cistern. The cistern sits right next to the spring, in the nearby forest, about three hundred yards from the main house.

Dave called while I was hosting a party in California.

"Leslie, I got some bad news for you. I went to check on your spring and the cistern is empty."

I asked if he could diagnose what was happening and he said he couldn't. I was twelve hundred miles away and helpless to handle the situation. All I could do was worry.

Now if you're not from the West, you won't understand this, but water is everything out here. Without water, you have a piece of dusty dirt that's worthless. Whole wars have been fought over water. I'd just plunked down my life savings on a piece of beautiful land, but without water I might as well have been throwing my money away.

I quickly arranged for my first extended trip to the cabin, driving to Wyoming in early May, and began the task of sorting out what was going on. Before arriving I'd talked with the previous owners who advised me to call Dan. Dan's the local deputy sheriff, but like everyone around here, he wears multiple hats. And one of those hats had to do with owning a backhoe and having some spring experience. At around 8 a.m. Dan knocked on my door. I explained I'd just bought this property and, although the owners told me my spring was running well, the cistern was virtually dry. Dan said a lot of springs are drying up, especially on the other side of the river, the south facing slopes. He helped get my pressure pump running, which was another problem I had in my December initial visit. Mostly he scratched his head and said he'd had his own water problems with his well running dry on his ranch.

That weekend my neighbor Ric, who shares rights on the

spring, arrived. His family uses the cabin intermittently, so he was unaware of the water problems. He and his dad built the spring catchment system in the 1980s. At that time they'd rented a backhoe and a ditch witch, and dug a trench through forest service land, from the spring to my house, then down the road another two hundred feet to their home, and installed PVC mainline six feet underground. In Wyoming six feet is the frost-free line. Another neighbor downhill also shared our spring. Three households were involved in our little Water Department. With the spring running one-half gallon per minute — not the fourteen gallons per minute the seller had told me — we could never supply all of us simultaneously.

Ric knows this system better than anyone else. Because I have an understanding of water and irrigation design, it didn't take much for him to explain the entire set-up and for me to understand it. So Ric and I trounced up to the spring and poked around. We opened up and peered into the cistern, really just a three-hundred-gallon plastic septic tank buried in the ground. Above the cistern the underground spring emerges from a large sinkhole. You can find these kinds of formations all around the area. They are easy to identify as their natural cavity is filled with water-loving plants.

Within this wet depression a collection system had been installed twenty years ago. A series of parallel pipes with holes in the bottom collected the water, moving it into the holding tank. The theory is the same as a landscape french drain which moves pooling water away from an area. Once in the cistern, a mainline pipe ran to all of our homes, gravity fed. Any excess water in the cistern exits via an overflow pipe at the top of the tank, back into the natural watercourse. Of course, not 100% of the water could be collected, so the stream should still have running water.

When we examined our situation, the spring was running just

fine but the cistern flow was less than one gallon a minute. The question was why?

Ric's brother, a geologist, had some theories:

Possibility# 1. Small earthquakes shifted the limestone layer and changed the direction of the springs

Possibility #2. The ten year drought has dried up our source. The mother spring is farther up into the forest, and as we are towards the end of the water line, with six springs higher up towards the source, we are no longer getting much water.

Possibility #3. The more recent development of a spring higher up from ours, on which we had no water rights, shifted some of the underground waterways that travel through the limestone.

Theories only. None of them sounded good to my ears.

I went back to the cabin, experiencing a not-yet-but-soon-to-be familiar feeling of helplessness, overwhelmed by the forces of nature. That night I had a strange dream, similar to my first night here last December. This time no people, no story, just an image of water and a voice-over that said *"Copious amounts of water."* I awoke feeling that some mysterious hand of help was intervening. Now I was certain: *That spring is not dry. It is either diverted or clogged.* And I hoped it was clogged.

I had my own theories. First I called the seller. He felt that the collection system, the pipes, could be faulty and clogged. At the other end of the forest was a spring permitted to the sellers' cousin. I called him for advice.

"A few years ago we went up to the cabin in the summer and the hoses were dry to the cabin. I took a shovel and started digging around the collection box. That's all it took to unclog some of the debris caught in there."

Although his system is set up different than mine, he confirmed the possibility of one of my hot theories — the clogged theory!

Since our entire water department was in tow, I was elected to don a pair of fisherman's pants and climb into the septic tank to check the input and output pipes. The water is all from snow-melt and the frigidity at the bottom of the tank didn't lie about that. It was decided that every morning for two weeks I would take a reading of the water level using a stick and check the gallons/per/minute output of the stream. I'd keep a chart and report back later.

I made a plan. First, I would put worry aside. Even though the ink was still wet on the escrow papers, I had reinforcements in the form of my neighbors. They too shared my concerns and we were all in this together. I decided to trust. Somehow things would work out. Second, I'd enjoy my two weeks here and explore my new digs.

I'd keep a chart and report back later.

The second pledge was simply a subheading under my first pledge. But third, I was going to do a little digging with a shovel, crack into the collection system and see if more water emerged.

Everyday I went to the stream, undid the cover on the cistern, measured the height of the water and took a reading. I made sure that it was the same time each morning, before I showered or used any water. One afternoon, a few days later, I was driving back home from a hike in the upper end of the valley. As I rounded a bend near the Forest Service cabins, a large badger surfaced from a hole. I stopped at a cattle guard and watched. He was right by the road and he also spent some time wondering what I was doing there. He eyed me suspiciously and I studied him with great satisfaction. I'd never actually seen a badger before, just their evidence. They tend to be nocturnal, emerging around dark and hunting by night, digging ground squirrels and gophers out of their holes for a meal. For me, this sighting was a rare treat.

The badger went back into his large hole. I too headed back home. The following evening I was on the phone trying to arrange some work on the house when I looked out my window and, lo and behold, there was another badger, this time appearing from a hole in the hillside. I had a badger living next to my house. I watched as he waddled off for his evening rounds.

Badgers are great diggers. The claws on their front feet are up to 1¾" long. The long claws loosen the soil and pass it backwards, while the hind feet throw the dirt 6-8 feet behind the digging animal. A badger den is quite elaborate, up to eight-feet deep and thirty-feet long. This main tunnel leads to an elevated chamber to discourage flooding. Another smaller chamber is used for a latrine. A badger den could contain several entrances and very old dens might have as many as forty exits.

I considered these rare two sightings back to back. I decided this animal was a symbol given to me by the land itself and a suggestion that what I needed to do was DIG for the *copious amounts of water*.

That next morning I started my digging task. As any one knows who creates something from nothing, the job of bringing an idea from the ethers into the manifest is always much harder than the mind imagines. And so it was with this endeavor. I had no idea how this catchment had been built nor how deep they'd gone. After twenty years, layers upon layers of soil and roots had built up. When they dug this out with a backhoe originally, large pieces of limestone rocks emerged. Working with these natural springs, I was told, one had to be very careful not to disturb the landscape too much. The springs move and change. They are a very delicate network that we humans don't fully understand and it's easy to disrupt their flow if you dig too fiercely and forcefully. So although initially they used machinery, they put their pipe and gravel in, then carefully laid all the limestone boulders back on top, creating a thick layer of rock.

I was digging with a shovel yet continuously hitting rock. When I wasn't hitting rock I was struggling with fibrous roots of sturdy plants like cow parsnip. I worked, little by little, over the course of a few days when suddenly, a large stream of water began to emerge! It was true, the lines were simply clogged and the solution was to dig out the old system and replace with new gravel and a more modern updated system of larger PVC drain pipe.

I had added a fourth item to my list. If this stream was to bring forth and give me its life energies, then I needed to reciprocate. Even though my drinking water entered the cistern before the spring emerged, my work with land over the years instilled in me a certain ethic: by honoring and bringing a special 'regard' for the land, a mutually beneficial relationship is created. The stream itself had become overgrown and full of dead limbs, downfall, and general refuse. I vowed to give time to restore its health and clean it up. It was my ceremony of service to the spring. Others might wonder why should I bother. I couldn't do much with the invisible, but I could serve the visible part of the stream. I'd created streams before in my work. I've sat and watched how they flow, how to make them look natural even when they are man-made in someone's back yard. It would be thrilling to work with this natural spring as a labor of love.

I spent time my first summer clearing fallen trees and hauling in new limestone to hold in the sides of the stream that had been displaced over time by cattle and horses trampling through the watershed. Now, every summer I make a point to do a little stream restoration work as a sacrament, an offering of thanks for the life-giving water that this stream supplies me with daily.

* * * * * *

If you explore the complete workings of this riparian area that lies between the marsh below and the dry hillside of fir and pine above, you notice how alive this area is. I've watched these springs for many years now. They are interesting, with a flow that varies unpredictably. Jack says they have their own logic, and that logic doesn't necessarily match the melt. Many times in the late spring the flow is quite low. When summer rolls around the flow picks up. The recharge is somewhere deep inside Mt. Herman, and not on an annual cycle. Whereas ground aquifers that dry out due to long droughts need several years of recharging for the water levels to rise, these springs operate differently. An almost record snowfall one winter didn't necessarily bring more water to the springs the following summer. In fact, the main spring that seems to feed all the others had less water in some wetter years. Who knows how the water moves underneath the upper tiers of limestone.

The seven springs that emerge through the hillside create marshy areas of meadow and willows on the private lands below. Eventually everything drains into Elk Creek, a refuge for resident moose. There is one spring in particular that I like to think of as the 'Mother Spring.' A huge circular depression, created by the massive weight of the underground water, sports water loving plants like Cow Parsnip (*Heracleum maximum*) and Red Baneberry (*Actea rubra*). An ancient concrete spring box is hidden underneath the overgrowth in the middle of the sinkhole, though it's not functional anymore. The large cavity mimics a natural amphitheatre.

Red Baneberry loves shady moist conditions

Arrowheads and other Indian artifacts have been found in these springs. I like to go to this particular sinkhole and imagine it's a place where water spirits, the *pandzoavits* of the Sheep Eaters, might be working their magic.

I was tickled that this sacred little forest contained exactly seven springs. In the mood of 'play,' I considered it was a spring for each chakra of the body. Eastern yogic tradition points out seven centers of the human body, and each center is called a chakra. All are important and if any are blocked they can cause disease: emotional, physical or psychic. The chakra system begins at the base of the spine, and follows the human body all the way to the top of the head, the highest chakra representing our connection to the source of all universal energy. Whether my spring is the root or the crown, just like the physical body, the health of this forest is dependent on

all of these springs flowing freely.

With its abundant supply of water and cover, the forest is a magnet for wildlife. It's also a corridor, or pass through, between several valleys and watersheds. Using my trail camera over the seasons, I've gotten to know some of the nocturnal goings-on. Wildlife, like humans, like routine. They follow general patterns and have their home ranges. You can also count on these patterns continually changing. One year a black bear will be making her rounds through the woods every two weeks, the next year I rarely see her.

On my trail camera I've caught black and grizzly bears, cougar, deer, elk, moose, wolves, coyotes, turkeys, bobcats, and plenty of small animals. Besides the variety of wildlife in such a small area, what amazes me is that I'll clock a deer at 4 p.m., then a cougar at 9 p.m. the same day; then a wolf at 6 a.m. and a coyote an hour later. One time I caught a wolf chasing a coyote. What's also interesting is how the animals are acting when they are photographed.

I'll clock a deer at 4 p.m., then a cougar at 9 p.m.

Sometimes they are running, other times they are at their 'baseline,' a relaxed posture that is different for each animal. I've caught a cougar running at top speed at 3 a.m. and I wonder — from what? Deer, move cautiously, slowly and warily at all hours. They munch, then look. Wolves seem to be passing through, returning from a night's work. Coyotes come at all hours of the day, are curious and wary as well. Bears, on the other hand, rule the roost, never seem to be in a hurry and display no fear in their posture.

One spring a winter-killed deer lay at the edge of the woods. In tough winters, many deer don't make it to the spring. I pulled out my trail camera, thinking this was a great opportunity, and attached it to a nearby tree. I waited a good two weeks. I didn't want to run into a hungry spring bear. The day before I decided to check the camera, a neighbor paid a visit. Larry was out from the mid-West for a few days to antler hunt. I asked where he'd been and how it had gone.

"We hiked up along the old irrigation ditch on Russell Creek. Wouldn't you know it some idiot hauled a road-killed deer way up there and put a trail camera on it? I'm gonna tell the game warden."

Russell Creek is far from these woods, but I wondered if there was a lesson here. Was I doing something illegal by putting my camera on the dead deer in my nearby woods? The deer Larry encountered was, I found out later, planted by the Interagency Bear scientists for their research. But neither he nor I knew this then. I asked Larry if that was illegal.

"Well, the deer would attract bears!"

That next morning I went to check the camera. The first thing I noticed was the carcass was gone and my camera's front completely smashed in, as if someone had taken a rock and pounded on it. Who would do such a thing? Remembering my neighbor's story, I thought maybe the game warden had come by, dragged the carcass away because it was too close to homes, and given me a good warning. It all seemed implausible but I was getting paranoid. I was taking the destruction done to the camera as a personal attack.

I looked around and found drag marks. I followed the drag marks up a steep deer trail along the hillside. *That game warden sure worked hard if he dragged the animal all the way up this slope.* I gave up the hike before I found the carcass. It was just too steep.

I opened the camera and found the chip still intact. *Maybe there are some clues here.* All the way back to the house I tried to figure out how the warden would even have known, or cared. *He really finds out about everything concerning animals in these parts, doesn't he?* No other homes are occupied on this side at this time of the year. Also, these little woods are landlocked; in other words, there is no vehicle access and just about the only way to get to them is through private properties, one of them being mine. I hadn't seen the warden in weeks. And why would he smash up the camera? I kept thinking I was in trouble, but why? My mind was abuzz.

I returned to the cabin with the chip and put it into the computer. As the pictures loaded, I found my culprit. The camera had been set to video mode. The first clip showed giant lips and a loud 'thunking' noise. In the next clip a nose appeared with some chewing noises. As the nose pulled away, you could see a big grizzly bear. It was a bear that ate my trail camera! I laughed at myself, and the next time I saw the warden I told him the story.

So what was my mistake? Why did that bear chomp down on my camera? I talked to my boss in the natural history lab at the local museum where I had begun to volunteer. He'd done his PhD study on bears and knew their habits well.

"You didn't wipe off the camera. Always wipe your camera. And use gloves to set it up, especially with a carcass there. That bear smelled you, and thought you were out for his meal."

However possibly the funniest series of photos I obtained was of a dispersing young female cougar. She'd been hanging around for a few weeks in the spring, and I had a new trail camera that flashed red when the infared light was on. As people with house cats know, felines are attracted to shiny things. To catch bobcats and cougars on film, biologists sometimes hang shiny metal objects. At first I caught several photos of the lion walking back and forth, in and out of the woods, eyeing the camera. Finally, she came right up to the camera, squatted and peed right in front of it, marking her territory and asserting her dominance over this strange flashing red light.

She peed right in front of it, marking her territory.

* * * * * *

Upon moving here, I walked through this little forest daily during the winter. I didn't just walk the trail, but waded through the private lands below the National Forest. The owners were all gone for the winter, and besides, I figured they'd like me keeping an eye on their properties for them. The forest on the private lands was a maze of springs, marsh, and dying or dead old growth Englemann Spruce. Some of these spruce were over two hundred years old, but the beetles were wrecking havoc, tunneling through their cambium layers. The sheer volume of beetles, without the cold winters we once had that knocked them back, overwhelmed the trees. These old giants couldn't pitch the beetles out fast enough and there just weren't enough woodpeckers in the entire basin to help them out. Their time was limited.

It seems there's a beetle for just about every conifer — Douglas-Fir beetle, Mountain beetle, Jeffrey pine beetle, Spruce beetle, Pinyon Ips, the list goes on. These Spruce beetles have a two-year cycle. Although the spruce beetle will attack all spruce, they prefer Engelmann. Infested spruce trees usually do not turn 'red-needled' until one or sometimes two years after the attack. Periodic beetle infestations are natural to the landscape, but what's been happening all over the West and Canada comes from a combination of the hundred-year policy of fire suppression, tight forests with older trees, prolonged drought and a warming climate. Beetles are highly sensitive to slight changes in their environment. Small shifts can create rapid, extreme shifts in outbreak. Warmer winter temperatures reduce cold-induced mortality and also create conditions where the beetles can reproduce more frequently — a virtual population explosion.

With the forest slowly dying, a large amount of debris and deadfall was collecting. Walking through these woods was no easy chore, winter or summer. But in the winter, the snows piled up making going even slower, and there were no trails except those the deer and moose had etched out.

Yet these interior woods interested me the most. There was a lot of life in there, hidden in the snarls and crags of the downed timber and what was left of large old growth standing trees. In the summer I'd found where the Great Horned Owl liked to roost. I'd collected his pellets and discovered all the kinds of voles he was eating. There were special places where the deer hid. I watched a moose give birth at the forest's edge and saw where the bears like to bed down. As the forest approached the county road, it gave way to willows, the ground becoming too saturated for even spruce. Those willows were the occasional abode of moose.

One evening near dusk, I was making my rounds through the woods. The light was dim when I decided to follow a deer run. I was almost crawling under some brush when I spotted droppings at the base of a snag. I bent down to get a closer look, and spooked a bird from the top of the debris. The bird flew to a nearby tree. I felt there was something unusual about this bird. I called Koda, who had accompanied me, and told him to lie down. Ever so slowly I crawled out from the tangle I was caught up in and peered into the low hanging spruce limbs.

It took a few minutes for my eyes to adjust to the evening light. At first the bird appeared to be a large robin. But robins migrate elevationally in the winter, going down into Cody or further south. No, this was no robin, but a small owl, about seven inches tall and just as curious about me as I was about him. I sat down on a log, watched and talked to the bird. He sat above my head. If I had stood up, we would have been just about eye-to-eye. I found an owl pellet beside the log, about half the size of a Great Horned pellet. This was this little guy's roost. The owl wasn't afraid at all. For over an hour, the owl and I communed together, while Koda fell asleep at the base of the tree. I could see why there is a lore about them being 'wise.' His eyes, big and beautiful, had an intensely calming affect on me. He was a gentle soul. As darkness fell, I felt it was time to let this little owl have his night to hunt. Besides, I had no flashlight and would have to stumble my way home.

Back at the house I looked up the owl's name — Northern Sawwhet. These little owls inhabit coniferous and deciduous forests, with thickets of second-growth or shrubs. They like to breed in swampy or wet areas, preferring riparian habitats. With plenty of

I could see why there is a lore about them being 'wise.'

thickets, downfall, and debris in which to hide from larger predators, plus the thickness of some of the young new trees, this owl
had a cozy and safe home.

This lower forest, with all the dying spruce, clearly could use
the helping hand of wildlands sustainable management. I had
envisioned piling and burning some areas, including a lot of the
deadfall, while systematically leaving certain dead snags to provide nesting and roosting areas. Without forest fires for so long, the
natural mosaic of the forest and meadows had become stilted. With
some thoughtful, careful snipping here and there, a more produc-
tive wildlife habitat could be gotten. There was even enough water
for a pond to attract migrating birds and more wildlife.

Soon I found the homeowners had been offered a deal by the
state: the state would help clean up the forest by providing 'x'
amount of dollars per acre for the logging and would even find the
loggers. Some of this is politics (good business for loggers), some of
it is fire management (easier and cheaper for the fire department to
clear areas preventatively around homes than to fight a forest fire)
and some came out of the persistent cries of the homeowners for
help. The intentions all around were good, but the results were literally messy, and in the short term, more of a fire hazard. The state
forester decided what would be best would be to cut everything
over 3-4" diameter or about forty years old and older. "They'll all
be dead in a few years anyways from beetle." That winter the loggers came in with heavy equipment, accumulating massive slash
piles but leaving plenty of debris on the forest floor. By the following winter, many of the trees that weren't cut were now blow
downs. The streams that went through the forests were trying to
establish new channels, but with all the trash of branches, blow
downs, sticks and limbs, the area was simply a marshy jumble, and

fairly denuded. Invasive weeds like Canada thistle and blue-bur overtook certain areas. Where my little Northern Saw-whet flew off to, I just have to wonder.

A tremendous amount of slash from the logging was dragged into my neighbor's meadow. The pile was as big as a two-story home: fifty feet long by fifteen feet high. There were limbs and trunks, but also huge entire logs many feet in girth. The logging was completed by the time I arrived home in January. And my new vista out my front window was of this enormous pile. Since that neighbor is absentee, I asked his permission to do the burn myself that winter.

That winter the snows were light, with few good days for this monster burn; we needed as much moisture and coolness in the air as possible. My friend Gary, an ex-forest fighter, was the main man for the job. One evening we awoke to a light snow and Gary pronounced,

"Let's burn. We'll start this evening when the humidity is higher."

With a good amount of diesel fuel, the pile torched easily. And once it got going, you couldn't stand closer than 150 feet away without feeling scorched. It looked like an entire forest was on fire. The pile burned like that all night. I was waking up every few hours just to look out the window; by 3 a.m. the pile was still a roaring blaze, lighting up the entire sky. The next morning people stopped at the side of the road to watch. I loved every minute of it. Fire has always come into my life. I've been the first to arrive at several house fires; I grew up next to a large park in Los Angeles where we had regular wild fires every summer. Even one summer as a child our neighborhood was evacuated when a large fire burned out of control. As a teenager I used to compete with my friends to see who could start a campfire with one match in the shortest period of time. Fire has always been a fascination for me and now I was witness to the fire of a lifetime — controlled, exhilarating — it was an academy award winning bonfire!

As a horticulturist, someone who has worked with land all my life, I couldn't help but imagine how I'd have managed that little forest differently. Certainly that little woods needed some help, but I'd have cleared in a slow rhythm, selectively thinning over the course of eight years or more. I'd expose new small patches of meadow, control the invasive thistle in these sunny areas (since the open areas would be small, there wouldn't be so many invasive weeds), and encourage new natives to take root. New meadows would be established when in the successive years dead trees were removed. I could selectively leave healthy aspens to establish new young groves (aspens root-clone themselves), and plant willows from pieces of cuttings. I could dig a pond to encourage water-fowl and other wildlife. I had restoration fantasies of that beautiful space. Instead, now I can't walk through the area without stepping in muck, slipping over slash, or seeing a large patch of invasive weeds.

It's been a few years since the forest logging. What's fascinating is the little woods on the Forest service lands are still intact and full of wildlife. That's where my trail camera sits and I continue to record wildlife passing through regularly. Animals like edges — where meadows meet forests for example. It allows browsers to browse when they want, but retreat to the forest for cover when necessary. Animals like to move through the cover of the woods.

The private lands logging was the first forest issue I encountered up here. On its heels came the new Forest Service proposals for this valley. After a few years of public comment, the Forest

Service will begin, this year, implementing over a period of eight years, their approved forest plan. There will be more logging and some burning, but mostly logging. I always prefer burning. Burning is nature's way of cleaning up. There are no stumps left, it clears out debris and forest duff, leaving room for fresh new seedlings to emerge quickly, and most importantly, the West is fire-adapted. This means that many plants and trees need fire to sprout. Ceanothus seeds can live in the soil up to two hundred years, requiring a heat treatment to break dormancy. After a fire, a succession of growth naturally follows. For the first forty years or so after a large fire, more sunlight is able to reach the forest floor, allowing smaller plants to grow alongside tree seedlings. Many of these plants are nitrogen-fixers, meaning they put nitrogen back into the soils rather than taking it out, paving the way for future healthy plant material. Although many small animals that can't take cover quickly in a large fire might die, few large mammals perish. In the 1988 fires in Yellowstone, 1.4 million acres burned throughout the ecosystem, including 793,880 acres — more than one-third of the surface area — of the Park, yet less than three hundred large mammals perished. The '88 fires of Yellowstone were of a scale, which occurs naturally every 250-400 years. Whereas a man-made control burn is a contained fire, performed under optimal conditions, and is within a limited amount of acreage.

When I heard the Forest Service was preparing a restoration plan for the valley, I immediately wanted to read it, and was most concerned about our spring area and the little woods accompanying it. The suggested plan for that area was cutting then burning the trees in place. The area couldn't be used as a timber sale because a logging road couldn't be constructed into swampy areas, but the Forest Service proposed using a bobcat for the job. I was appalled.

Ric and I set up a meeting with the forest service hydrologist, archaeologist and planner to walk the spring area. We showed them where buffalo skulls had been pulled out and obsidian points found. We pointed out that these springs are delicate areas and cutting trees could alter the flows. We noted that we were afraid heavy equipment, even a bobcat, could cause compaction and reduce stream flow. Although all the spruce trees were dead and dying streamside, the hillside above — where the springs emerged — still had healthy stands of Douglas firs. We wanted to keep it that way. Please, let the forest, at least *here*, take care of itself. In the end, the Forest Service listened to the homeowners' pleas and left the area alone.

Walking a natural area everyday is good meditation. You learn a lot about the rhythms of the animals, the plants, the forces of nature. I can walk this little forest and still make discoveries each time. Where is the owl roosting this year; can I identify every plant in every season; are the moose still using this route; are the juncos coming back to nest in these thickets? Although I'm a hiker, this forest has taught me how much can be learned by slowing down, by inspecting the micro areas. I've learned that I don't need to hike miles and miles for discoveries; that the real discoveries are right under my nose. Extraordinary wildlife interactions are going on before my eyes, if I just stay alert and aware. Animals seem to choose if *they* want to be seen. In order for me to choose to see *them*, I must slow down and be alert to different signs. The crackling of leaves, the hollow sound of the earth, the alarm calls of the juncos and sparrows, a flash of movement out the corner of my eye — this is a new awareness for me. This little forest has been my teacher.

"And my experience has left no doubt in my mind but what there is some kind of telepathy between man and brute as well as man and man."

William H. Wright

CHAPTER 7

Bear Dreamers

Hibernation

It was the fall of 2010 and my third winter at the cabin. The first two winters I'd been in the Bay Area November through January. First, because I was 'trying to adapt,' mostly afraid of the prolonged isolation and the moxie it might take to make it through a full Wyoming winter, especially at 7,000 feet. I'd lived all my life on the California coast. Winters with snow were still foreign to me. Besides, I still needed the income I generated there.

Usually I'd rent temporary housing for that short span of time. But with this year's workload uncertain, I planned to stay with friends. While I worked on the jobs I was already contracted for, I thought I'd see if I could round-up additional ones. Yet this was to be the year I'd be forced to fully let go — of the security of my past, and the comfortable familiarity of mild winters. When I scheduled my winter trip to California, what I hadn't anticipated was how sick I'd be feeling.

In early September I backpacked into the Wind Rivers. For five years I'd been saving a portion of Soona's ashes. Long ago I'd divided her ashes into thirds — a third for California where she'd spent her life, a third for my Wyoming home, and the last third I'd saved for the Wind Rivers where she'd accompanied me on many trips. The summer was almost past, the season for high alpine hiking slipping away. I just had to get back for that ceremonial scattering.

I chose a southern route starting at Big Sandy, then north to Shadow Lake behind the famous Cirque of the Towers. The weather started off brilliantly clear and slightly crisp with fall in the air. I camped at Dad's Lake, planning to dayhike the ten miles roundtrip to Shadow Lake the next day. The following morning snow flurries and a heavy cloud cover cast an ominous mood over my excursion. I had the ashes wrapped in a plastic bag, and carried just enough supplies for a lunch and a possible overnight if the weather worsened.

There are actually three lakes at the mountains' base, stairstepping up to Texas Pass. Shadow, the lowest, sits at 10,287 feet, at the foot of Wolf's Head, Shark's Head, and other peaks rising over 12,000 feet. These lakes are situated at the end of a wide, high valley. Following the meandering Washakie Creek through stunted

Koda and I in the Winds

willows, the open valley weaves through spruce and whitebark pines. Leftovers of summer wildflowers and grasses pepper the valley in early September as it narrows up to the timberline basin. At the foot of this grand array of towering granite domes and spires lies Shadow Lake. A fitting place for my dog, I thought. Few people venture into the wonderland scenery of the backside of the Towers. Most travelers are climbers who approach from the west. On this snowy day, I had the valley and Washakie Creek all to myself.

The lake is fringed by erratic boulders and meadows. Crisscrossing the shallow stream several times, I made my way to the lake shoreline. I found a small clearing amidst the thick willows near the lake and pulled out the wrappings containing the ashes. As ceremoniously as I could, I scattered Soona's ashes, then found a rock to sit on for a few moments of prayers and remembrances. As soon as I sat down, the sun appeared through a small parting in the dark sky. Except for a tunnel of light directly above me, all was grey. The heat of the sun changed the mood of the moment. It was as if the heavens had opened to receive my prayers and Soona acknowledged her final resting place as *'Good.'* I started back to camp, the dark clouds closed in again, and it began snowing heavily.

It stormed all night. I was waking on and off to my shivering pup, Koda, who was sleeping under the tent vestibule. As the snow settled around the tent, I had a vivid and prescient dream about a bear. This bear dove into a swimming pool. He, or she, swam deep and was obviously enjoying his underwater swim. The expectation was that I would follow. I hesitated. What if the bear wanted to harm me? There was apprehension, and fear. Then I decided to follow. The dream ended with that decision, with me still standing at the edge.

* * * * * *

For thousands of years over the northern hemisphere world-wide, bears have held great meaning for people. Bears are omnivores like we are; they are excellent at using their hands to pick berries or use their 'digging stick' claws to find roots. They have a footprint akin to a human foot, are curious about their world, and move about their environment like a hunter-gatherer, venturing where foods are found seasonally. Female bears are protective and caring mothers, a trait humans admire. They give birth to nearly naked, helpless young in their winter dens, and the young stay with their mothers for two and a half years. A bear, dead and skinned, looks eerily like a human being.

Ancient peoples felt bears taught them how to hunt, but also which plants to eat — roots, seeds, grains, fruits, berries, nuts, stems, and mushrooms. Bears were the master plant gatherers of the animal world. Bears also ate most of the plants that tribes around the world gathered for medicines. Some of these medicinal plants were principal bear food. Therefore, bears were associated with herbal healing. They were the Medicine Healers. The bear spirit held the power to heal, and tribal healers sought its favor, through vision and dreams. Bears were 'humans without fire.'

One of the most striking and powerful features of bear life is their ability to hibernate. In late fall or early winter, bears begin to seek out their den site. They somehow know when the best time is and so begin their physical and physiological preparations. Grizzly bears, the digging bears, will more often excavate a den. Black bears may also dig but tend to den in rock crevices and under stumps and boulders. Bears may even build nests in the den, hauling chewed off boughs of spruce or fir to make a comfortable bed.

Ancient peoples observed bears disappearance coinciding with winter and their reemergence in the spring. Because bears spent half their lives underground in a death-like sleep, and emerged into a fresh new world in springtime, indigenous peoples associated them with transformation, death and rebirth, healing and initiation ceremonies, puberty, and shamanic secret societies. Just as hibernation began with retreat to a den, initiation began with the novice's separation and retreat to the forest, or another isolated place; and just as the bear in the den, the neophyte took no water or food. The candidate died and was reborn, as the bear entered the rebirth of the world in the spring.

* * * * * *

After my trip to the Winds and the bear dream still fresh in my mind, I came home to a fall filled with bear sign. Bears are always hungry in the fall. It's their time of hyperphagia, when their bodies are crazy for food, preparing for a long sleep in winter dens. They need to put on as much fat as they can.

The year 2010 was a lean one for bears. Although the ecosystem has an estimated 80% of its' whitebark pines functionally dead, this year's nut crop on the remaining live trees was poor. Combined with late spring snows, this made for difficult fall foraging. When a dream comes to conscious fruition, it is said the dreamer has 'found his dream.' Unknowingly, I was to initiate the process of 'finding' my bear dream. I began tracking a particular black bear who'd been visiting my property. I wanted to know him, his movements, what he'd been eating. I observed how he'd dug up dozens of limber pine middens the squirrels had collected. A midden is a refuse as well as a stash pile. The middens around here are squirrel caches of pine nuts. Squirrels build these up for years and years, caching new cones within the accumulating refuse of the old eaten cones and scales. The moisture in the deeper layers inhibits the new cones from opening, helping ensure the squirrels' winter larder is protected from thieves like mice and birds who have a hard time opening closed cones. Since squirrels are hoarders, caching up to thousands of cones, enough to feed a squirrel for years, hungry bears search out these middens. The proportion of seed to cone is much less for limber than for whitebark pine, as well as the thickness of the seed coats is greater for limber pine. More work for a bear for less payoff. Yet nutritious and rich with fat, these limber pine nuts were a decent substitute during poor whitebark pine years. A good crop of rose hips also produced an abundance of another favorite food. And of course, the occasional gut pile from a hunter's kill, a few of which were around my area.

One evening after following this bear's sign through thick aspen, I walked back home along my driveway. A large coil of used

Grizzly napping in the willows, camouflaged

barbed wire, usually stored along a side ditch, was sitting in the middle of the road. I inspected the wire and noticed bear fur. The bear in his roaming around must have gotten tangled, then dragged the roll of wire until he was loose. I tried to haul the wire out of the roadway but couldn't make it budge. That roll must have weighed seventy-five pounds. Another day, a huge log blocked my driveway. The log had rolled down a steep embankment. Looking up, I noticed where it had come from: a gargantuan old midden at the top of the hillside. This hungry bear had pawed his way through large tree stumps to dig deep into the squirrel's storage house. The midden was completely ravaged. A squirrel chattered away at me. "I'm not your culprit," I told her. These two incidents, the barbed wire and the log, left me with a sense of awe at the power of this bear.

I was spending several days a week backtracking the bear through nearby forest and fields. I observed his scat. It was usually dry with pine nut shell remains and rose hip seeds. I wondered how he could be getting enough nutrition and fat from rose hips. When a hunter killed a deer and left the gut pile on the main road, I rejoiced as I knew this hungry black bear would have some precious meat to eat. In my ramblings I was cautious. Certainly I didn't want to personally encounter the bear, only observe its wanderings and thinkings.

Because it was fall, I was occasionally seeing other bear sign, as well as having a few bear sightings from safe distances. I also was hearing stories from hunters. Hunters in particular risk confrontations with bears. They sneak around the woods at dawn and dusk; they bugle, imitating elk calls; and of course they kill deer and elk during the months when bears are in hyperphagia preparing for their long death-like sleep. Around these parts you often hear the saying, 'A hunter's gunshot is a bear's dinner bell.'

One October day during my weekly visit to town, I ran into my neighbor at the grocery store. They own a large ranch and bears sometimes venture into the hayfields in the fall. She told me her son heard a noise on the porch of his cabin the previous night. He looked out and saw a sow grizzly and three cubs.

Although I'd seen no sign of these four bears, I doubled my attention-efforts, keeping my bear spray close by. I also kept Koda on a shock collar, just to make sure he didn't run off too far from me. There's a lot of controversial and contradictory advice about bears and dogs. I took my cues from Trent, one of the interns on the elk study, who had spent time training Karelian Bear dogs. Karelian Bear dogs are used in many Canadian National Parks to teach grizzly and black bears to recognize and avoid human boundaries. Trent's first winter on the job, while he was going to school in Montana, he trained the dogs. The following summer he took the dogs into the field in Canada.

"There's not much to training these dogs with bears. That part's instinctual. What I did over the winter was take them to kills and reward them. If you want Koda to find kills," Trent told me, "then let him chew on the bones he finds. That's his reward."

The following winter when he returned from his first summer of fieldwork in Canada with the dogs, I asked him how it went. I was curious because many local people said dogs were a detriment when it came to bears. "They'll bring the bear back to you." Others told me they were good protection. What was the real scoop? I thought Trent would know.

"I had a crazy incident with a grizzly last summer," Trent told me. "We heard about a bear in a camping area, so I headed out there in the truck with my dog. I let the dog out and he found that bear. The bear was running through the woods in circles, with the dog chasing him. The bear would come around and when my dog showed up behind him, I'd call her, but she'd just make another circle after that bear. I was afraid I'd lose my dog. It was crazy, but finally the bear took off in the woods and here comes the dog, happy as a clam.

"Look, Leslie, as long as you keep Koda fairly close and under voice control, you'll be perfectly safe. You're much better off with the dog than without. That bear will run off once he sees your dog. It's just a matter of keeping Koda close to you. People let their dogs run all over the place in bear country. Then when the dog sees a bear, the dog runs back to the human. That's when people get in trouble. Koda's a great dog, well-trained. You'll be fine."

Little did I know I'd soon get to put his advice to the test. It was the end of October and my birthday. It was near dusk and I was in the meadows next to my house. Since I was only a few hundred yards from the house, searching around the meadows for Koda's tennis ball, I didn't have any bear spray with me. As I walked along the meadow, something caught my attention in my peripheral vision. A stump that, like so many stumps, looked like a bear. Usually I paid no attention to those stumps. But something compelled me to look further. And there was that sow grizzly with her three cubs. These were last year's cubs, and they were enormous — almost as big as their mother. All four bears were quietly feeding in the woods about seventy-five yards away. Strangely, they hadn't noticed me nor the dog, nor had the dog noticed nor smelled them. I called Koda and began slowly, deliberately, walking in the direction of the cabin, keeping mama and the cubs in sight. I was getting pretty close to the house, about two hundred feet away, when Koda realized we were heading back so soon. He began to balk, crying and jumping. It was then, when I had to reprimand the dog, that Mama Grizzly took notice of us.

She looked up and I could sense that a tension filled her. You could feel what was going on in her mind, that split second of indecision to protect her cubs — "Flight, or Fight?" I handled the dog, continuing towards the house, all the while keeping the bears in my peripheral view. Within seconds the mother decided we weren't a threat; with her cubs she loped towards the forest. I got back to the house with just enough time to get a fuzzy photo of the three cubs before they disappeared into the woods.

Safe at the house, I too had a tension filling me. My heart was pounding. Caught between breathlessness and excitement, nothing prepares you for that moment when you confront great power, and survive! That mama was close enough that if she had wanted, she could have been upon me in seconds. Yet I was also thrilled. I'd just seen four bears — a family of bears. What a sighting that was!

A few days later I went to check what those bears were digging for at this time of year. That Mama had to feed three hungry one and a half year old cubs. Those bears weren't digging middens, but digging up thistle roots. The following fall this mama returned, now alone and pregnant. She was working on the chokecherry bushes down at the end of the driveway. For five nights, every night, she spent an hour or two sitting on her haunches, deftly pulling cherries from the branches. Then she'd stand on her massive hind legs to grab a tall branch and bring it towards her.

After tracking bears intensively all fall, a strange thing started to occur. Although it might sound odd, as I lay down to sleep one night, I sensed what one might call 'bear consciousness,' or the Spirit of the Bear. I felt immersed in Bear Mind, a place without words but only feelings, sensations. Bear consciousness had a mustiness to it, full of smells that filled and guided the daily road map of their amblings and goings-on. Surely, through combining oneself with an animal, it is possible to communicate directly with them; to touch their world; to walk across transparent borderlines into a Mind where there are no limitations of form and shape. David Rockwell says in *Giving Voice to Bear:* "When someone [in a native culture] had a strong relationship with his or her guardian spirit, the spirit's presence was palpable to everyone, but the person who possessed the spirit felt it most keenly."

One person who touched that bear presence was William Wright. Wright was a grizzly hunter in the late 1800's. He tracked grizzlies for days at a time on foot across wild uncharted country. He carried just his one shot Winchester rifle, seeking them out and never drawing them in with baits. He believed in a hunt that pitted his own ingenuity, skills and craftiness against the bruins. Over time his respect for their intelligence led him to put down his rifle and take up photographing and writing about grizzlies with the intention of saving them from extinction. He was a hunter turned naturalist who'd tracked and watched hundreds of grizzly bears over his lifetime. His observations about these bears are revealing. Wright describes grizzlies not as ferocious and confident, but instead as wary and cautious, stopping frequently to smell or look for danger, "an inoffensive minder of his own business, 'defensive, not aggressive.'"

One story illustrates their extreme cautiousness and intelligence. By 1906 grizzlies were all but extinct in the Rockies, so Wright went to Yellowstone Park to use his new camera equipment. His was essentially the first 'trail camera'. He employed a sewing thread as a trip wire. One end he attached to an electric switch which exploded a flash and sprung the shutter of his camera. The other end of the thread was tied to a small stake driven into the ground beyond the trail. He located a heavily used bear trail, set up the apparatus, then hid in the bushes from dusk well into late evening to watch. Night after night, the bears that came bye all stopped to investigate the well- hidden thread, then retreated without tripping the flash. Many explored the thread up to the switch and down to the stake before taking off.

In one case, three bears who Wright had seen on a trail in the Canyon area (he was now over in Lake) approached the wire.

"I recognized them easily by the markings on the shoulder and neck of one of them. I may say here in passing, if it surprises any one to speak of recognizing a bear previously encountered, that there is … as much individuality in bears as in people, and that it is perfectly easy for me to recognize a grizzly once seen and closely examined, and under such circumstances as I am here describing I could tell a newcomer the moment he came into sight on the trail. These three bears came up to the spot where the wire was stretched, took one good sniff, and appearing to recognize it as the same outfit with which they already had experience, turned unconcernedly to their right and passed by on the other side."

Lacking any photographic success and thinking that these Yellowstone bears might be adapted to human presence, Wright walked up and down his selected trail several times in order to scent it and replaced his thread with an extremely thin filament. This he laid across a trail covered in tall grass, then stood behind a tree for the evening to watch. Wright describes the antics of each bear that approaches. Each one, old or young, sow or boar, again takes time to smell the wire and investigate. A group of three bears, different from those above, approach the wire.

"The leader stopped abruptly, and the three then stood up, looked at each

other knowingly, and then, for all the world as though they inferred a connection between my scent and the presence of the wire, began methodically to track me. I was standing near a tree, and, not having expected any such move on their part, I had not taken the precaution to step back out of sight, and now I did not dare to move for fear of frightening them. They followed my scent as a hound follows a hare and when within fifty feet of me, as I did not move a muscle, they seemed unable to make out whether I was a living object or an inanimate one, and they again moved cautiously forward, still in absolute silence. When about twenty-five feet away, they again stood up and examined me intently, evidently doubting whether I were a bona-fide stump. Here, indeed, would have been a glorious opportunity, had I had a camera in hand. But they had come as far as they cared to. Dropping silently on to all-fours, they suddenly abandoned their investigations and bolted."

Without having such direct and repeated experiences with grizzlies, it's impossible for a person in today's world to intimately understand their nature as Wright does. So instead, tales get told and assumptions are made, and what hikers and hunters have to go on is what we're taught to do in case we actually run into a bear. Usually this involves a gun or bear spray, making lots of noise, and retreating slowly. It's a one shot, all-in-one manual to staying safe and includes the presumption that seeing a grizzly means danger. And although these may be appropriate rules for us occasional explorers of wilderness, it leaves little room for understanding the true nature of these bears.

* * * * * *

Bears aside, throughout the fall I was becoming sicker and sicker. I was certain it was from the water; during my trip to the Winds my water purifier had been malfunctioning and sheep were coming off the mountain in the fall. Despite my insistence that I had a parasitic infection, doctors in Cody weren't treating me for one as the symptoms weren't 'classic' they said. And so by the time I arrived in California in early December, I'd been ill off and on for at least three months. I knew the medical ropes in my old haunts, and soon I received the proper treatment. Yet because I'd had Giardia for such a long time, my guts were still 'broken.' I was too ill to work and, needing to cocoon and heal, I cut short my time in California and drove home to Wyoming before Christmas. What had been set in motion in the Winds conspired to keep me in place for my first *full* winter here. And what a winter it was to be. The winter of 2010-2011 would bring record snows, in some places 600% of normal! Many people told me they hadn't seen snow like this since the epic winter of 1978-1979.

I lived through that Wyoming winter, experiencing a death and rebirth inside the den of my little cabin. My driveway filled up with snow and iced over so many times that my snow blower couldn't keep up. Sometimes I just left my car on the road, and used my sled, pulling the groceries up the long windy driveway to the house. My car got stuck five miles down the county road and I had to ski home. Dozens of peoples' cars were caught in snowdrifts on our road. Even the sheriff had to be pulled out one morning by the ranch hands. And on an evening when it was twenty below zero, I took a mug of boiling water outside, threw it into the night air, and watched the water turn to steam mid-stream.

The next spring, after such an intense winter, an abundance of winter-killed deer fed hungry bears. And just as mysteriously as the bears emerged from the earth, I too emerged from my winter den that spring, renewed and healed from my water sickness, and firmly rooted to my new home.

Emergence

I set up my trail camera in a place where I knew bears waking up from their long winter sleep passed through. A set of fresh, perfect grizzly tracks in the snow told me this bear was headed to a nearby ranch. The tracks were solid ice, perfectly clear, like an ice sculpture of grizzly paws sunk into the ground. I was mulling over how they turned into ice. *Maybe he walked here in the evening over thin snow, his body's heat then melted that snow, which then iced over.*

Every year in the early spring, the same grizzly frequents first the campground, searching for a meal left by careless campers. Then he moves across the dirt road into the ranch meadows. I chatted with Tim, the ranch wrangler. Tim said this grizzly walked right through the cows, looking for the mineral lick they usually leave out. But no lick was out this spring. "But he's still looking for it."

The ranch hands in this upper area of the valley always had some good grizzly tales. Once a ranch manager told me the Game & Fish were collaring on part of the ranch's property, so they invited him to have his picture taken next to the head of the sedated bear. I wasn't surprised when Tim told me another good grizzly story and I knew I'd be jealous all over again.

"You remember last year they were trapping and collaring. They caught three grizzlies on our property all in one morning. These traps are fifty-five gallon barrels. The bear goes in for the meat and the door closes behind him. The doors on both ends are simple metal grates.

"Well, Mark Bruscino (*the Game and Fish bear management specialist in Wyoming*) was there and asked if I wanted to come see something unusual. They'd never trapped three bears all at once. They had two sows and one cub, so it was going to be interesting to which bear the cub belonged. They trap the bears, then dart them with a light sedative. Mark said to me 'Look inside this barrel at that grizzly,' so I looked. And that bear, instead of looking out the grate, was looking sideways at the wall of the can. I looked from one end, then I looked from the other end. But each time I looked, the bear looked away, as if she was shy or something.

"'What's going on?' I asked Mark.

"'That bear is embarrassed,' he said. 'She's been caught before and she's embarrassed that she got caught again.'

"Then Mark sedated her and looked at her ear tag. 'That bear, Mark said, was the first bear he'd ever caught and collared, eleven years back. She was three years old then.

"She'd only been handled by people twice, both of them himself.

"'She remembers me. Bears are smart. Most people would be shocked to learn how smart bears are.' Mark told me."

Tim was getting more excited as he recounted his story. He leaned over close and began almost whispering, as if telling me one of his special secrets.

"You know, bears can hear you when they're sedated. Mark, he was talking to that bear saying things like 'Hi, you remember me.' She'd be sure to remember something like being caught in a trap.

"Mark told me that bear had been in Dubois, caught and transferred for cattle killing. She was put in our valley and didn't get into any trouble for all those years, until last year when she killed our pigs. A year later she was tracked by her GPS collar down in Dubois again, but since then the collar's fallen off. When you think about it, how does a bear know, after being trapped in Dubois, then flown here by helicopter, not even driven here, but flown…how can they know how to get back to Dubois. That's maybe 150 miles from here and they don't go the same route. She had to cross three highways, and it's really rugged country between here and there. I asked Mark about that and he said those strong homing instincts help to maintain a certain balance and order in the bear population.

"Well we had about half hour before those bears woke up. I helped Mark pull them out of the cans. I was trying to be really gentle so as not to twist her paw or whatever. Mark laughed and told me there's no handles on the bears, you just pull on their fur. 'Don't worry about hurting them.' He said. 'These are massive creatures. They've been over rock cliffs and in all kinds of situations.'"

I had actually met Mark Bruscino several years previously on an organized field trip about grizzlies in our area. Mark, Chris Servheen (the grizzly bear recovery coordinator for U.S. Fish and Wildlife Service) and I drove up the North Fork where trout were

spawning, hoping to see some bears. On the ride up Mark talked about moth sites and the wonder of bears. Army cutworm moths migrate by the thousands from the prairie up to 300 miles to feed on alpine wildflowers. Bears disappear sometime early July, moving high up to feast on these moths, which congregate under rocks in great

numbers. The moths provide critical fat for their hibernation later in the fall.

I asked about moth sites and told him that I'd once seen one in the Wind Rivers.

"The Winds are great habitat for bears. There are a lot of moth sites there. Still some viable white bark pines there too. A lot of the high country outside Cody has good moth sites. Just in the last few years we've identified more than fifty possible moth feeding sites.

"Bears are amazing. They remember; their sense of smell is superb. They can work the wind, smelling food from miles away. And if they find a food reward, they'll remember it and come back to that place over and over again. Behaviorists rank grizzly bears in terms of intelligence up there with the Great Apes."

I remembered a backcountry hunter's camp I came upon several years back. The hunters had cut logs and tied a makeshift corral for their horses. They'd drunk beer and stayed for several days. Maybe they'd been coming here for several years in a row. Their campsite was filthy. They thought everything in the world would burn, so they'd thrown all their trash into the firepit. Of course, glass and tinfoil don't burn. I spent time cleaning it all up, dismantling the corral, and packing all the garbage out.

The next summer on the same hike, I was curious if the hunters had returned. I looked the site over, but it was as clean as I'd left it. What wasn't the same was the enormous quantity of fresh — several hours old at the most — bear scat everywhere. The bear had even defecated right on the log next to where all the trash had been. I really got the feeling that this bear knew this campsite and was coming around looking for easy food. There were so many scat piles that I wondered how many bears could there have been there. I posed the question to tracker Jim Halfpenny who conducts track classes inside the Park.

"I have seen bears feeding on rich grass sites use the same latrine repeatedly and create a large pile. Bears at carcasses often leave a lot of scat in a small area. Perhaps this site was being treated in a similar manner. Probably possessively."

Even though it had been over a year since I cleaned it up, bears never forget.

"Where you live, there's gotta be a grizzly up every drainage," Mark tells me.

We discuss all the bears that have been moved to my area, the 'bad' bears who get their first or second strikes by killing livestock and getting into people's garbage. Bears don't get past a third strike.

"It's not the problem bears you have to worry about. Tell your neighbors they'll be gone within a few days. It's the resident bears you need to watch out for."

The restoration of the grizzly bear back from the brink is a testament to how the Endangered Species Act is supposed to work.

* * * * * *

The restoration of the grizzly bear back from the brink to a healthy population is a testament to how the Endangered Species Act is supposed to work. As the numbers of bears increase in the Greater Yellowstone Area, the talk of delisting and hunting, intensifies. Recently grizzly bears were delisted, but just as soon as they were delisted, a court order relisted them. The Interagency Grizzly Bear Study Team, a group of state and federal officials, is tasked with determining whether white bark pine decreases will severely impact the grizzly population in the Greater Yellowstone Ecosystem (GYE). White bark pines, a species of tree that can live for a thousand years, are dying, succumbing to a host of attacks, from blister rust to beetles to climate change. They are already declared functionally extinct in the Greater Yellowstone area, with over 80% dead in the ecosystem. In my area alone, I have estimated that over 90% of the mature white barks are dead, although young trees are coming up, especially in older burn areas. This required study will be completed by 2014, when state agencies as well as the federal government are pushing for delisting.

The GYE is full to grizzly bear carrying capacity. Grizzly bear habitat needs to expand. Every time a grizzly either moves into territory not outlined as reintroduction habitat, or gets into trouble with livestock, he is moved: from Jackson to Crandall, Crandall to Dubois, Dubois to Gardiner. After three incidents, the bear is usually euthanized. Grizzlies are in a virtual zoo-park, with the visible lines showing on maps that bears can't read.

The not-to-delist argument is that the bears' main food sources — cutthroat trout and pine nuts — are drying up and disappearing and climate change is a big unknown for the bear. The delist argument is that grizzlies have recovered. State wildlife biologists say grizzlies are smart, they'll adapt to the absence of these critical foods by finding new ones. There is agreement on both sides that the Greater Yellowstone habitat is becoming full. Delisting takes the view that the Greater Yellowstone Ecosystem is the beginning and end of the area where bears around here can live; therefore they should be delisted and hunted to be 'managed' within carrying capacity for the ecosystem. Keeping them on the Endangered and Protected List argues that we don't know the future for these bears in the GYE.

Whatever the decision on delisting, Greater Yellowstone should not be the artificial limit of grizzly territory. Delisting arguments only consider the initial bear recovery zone (known as the Primary Conservation Area or PCA). Research shows that although the Yellowstone population is relatively healthy now, if these bears remain isolated, the population may eventually die out. For long-term health and genetic diversity, the population must contain several thousand bears, with landscape connectivity. This requires several tasks: expanding their population south into the Wind River Range (as well as including these southern regions in the Primary Conservation Area mandate); working to recover bears in the Selway-Bitterroot forest of Montana (this area expanded is referred to as the Central Idaho Complex, currently unoccupied by grizzlies); and connecting ecosystems north and south from the Central Idaho Complex to source populations in Canada.

The U.S. Department of Agriculture runs a Sheep Experiment Station with 2,000 head of sheep on 16,000 acres of land high up in the Centennial Mountains. The Centennials are considered an important connective corridor for grizzlies (and other wildlife) as they connect Yellowstone Park to large wilderness tracts in the

Idaho Complex. Putting sheep in this area creates conflict with wildlife passage; the Sheep Station needs to be retired.

A University of Alberta study concluded that grizzly extinction in the U.S. would be greatly reduced if a healthy population of bears occupied the Central Idaho Complex. To do this, grizzlies need room to roam. They need large amounts of space to obtain food. They need continuous tracts of land to move along corridors up and down suitable habitat.

The last several years in the GYE has been tough on bear-human

The Primary Conservation Area

Large Lakes (> 1 square mile)
Bear management Unit Boundaries
Subunit Boundaries
Yellowstone National Park Boundary

5 0 5 10 15 Miles

conflicts. Yellowstone saw its first fatality in over twenty years, with two deaths in one season. The year before, a mother grizzly with three cubs pulled a sleeping man from a tent in the middle of the night, killed and consumed him in a campground by the Northeast entrance — a clear predatory bear. When the analysis came back from DNA and the autopsy report on the bear, oddly enough she had been almost completely vegetarian for the last four years, eating a fully natural diet with no human foods. She had three underweight cubs and was trying to feed them. Her own condition was described as "thin". Since this is such a rarity, one has to ask: Was this bear desperate to feed her three cubs with an inadequate food supply in the ecosystem?

The year 2011 saw two summer deaths in Yellowstone — one was a mother defending her cubs while the other death is unclear. In the second death a tourist day-hiked into an area where there is no overnight camping due to high grizzly use. His body was found several days later. At least nine grizzly bears were feeding on two bison carcasses in the area, including one carcass that was 150 yards from where the body was found. Sixteen bear daybeds were also found in the vicinity. Neither of these two victims was carrying bear spray.

Bears, and grizzly bears, carry risks for humans in the back-country. But so does the act of driving a car. The upshot of these attacks isn't that bears need to be confined more, but they need more room to roam and expand. Thanks to dedicated people and the Endangered Species Act, the Great Bear has made a resounding comeback. We almost lost him just thirty years ago. And so the ecosystem that the grizzly is protected within — and therefore confined within — has gotten too small to feed all the bears. Starving grizzlies that are over-populated, whose food sources are compromised, will go for whatever they need to eat in order to survive. Giving them more room to find food, decreasing their population concentrations, may make things safer for humans, not the opposite.

We are at another crossroads with the Great Bear. For the bear to survive with enough genetic diversity, we must begin to think bigger and broader. Yellowstone to Yukon (Y2Y) is the name for an extensive wildlife corridor that will give these large mammals a chance to move and find food as well as new mates. The idea here is to provide connectivity of habitat for wildlife to move north and south easily. The Y2Y region encompasses 502,000 square miles, five U.S. states, two Canadian provinces, and two territories. Federally protected lands already occupy 10% of the Y2Y area. The remainder needs to be preserved through conscious and intentional planning.

Public lands are separated by private populated valleys. Private forested lands are being populated rapidly, and randomly, with no planning in place for wildlife or even for visuals. Besides connectivity issues, highways and new road building can physically bar movements of bears. All of this human encroachment has been studied and well-documented to have a disruptive influence on wildlife. The strategy goals of the Yellowstone to Yukon Conservation Initiative are tangible and practical: all major transportation routes permeable to wildlife; 75% of the people living in the Yellowstone to Yukon region knowledgeable about bears and more than 50% using bear-proof containers; 17,000 to 20,000 grizzly bears in the Y2Y region; and a significant reduction in the number of proposals for large scale recreational and industrial developments in grizzly-bear habitat. Humans will need to not only thoughtfully set-aside corridors, but accept living with top predators like bears in these human-wildlife interface areas. The act of connecting some of these large last wild tracts requires the best in us.

Scientists have known that one of the main ways species go extinct is through a process called 'islandization,' pockets of isolated habitat where plant and animal species are severed from genetic diversity. Pollinators can't move from one isolated area to another so plants go extinct. Animals have no 'bridges' (wildlife corridors) to find food or breed, the lifeblood of genetic diversity. The Y2Y corridor is one of the world's few remaining diverse landscapes, geographically and biologically, with the potential to help stressed species adapt to a changing climate. Instead of just preserving species, conservation groups are now thinking more about preserving mixed habitats, admitting that no one knows what wildlife will be needing in this new unpredictable climate. Conserving critical habitats and linking them with ecologically meaningful corridors would at the very least allow the continuation of long-term ecological and evolutionary processes.

Regeneration

Our neighborhood this summer was delighted and amused at the chance to follow a black bear cub's antics and wanderings. He appeared about three springs old, obviously newly kicked out by his mother. He visited the nearby ranch, peeking into the windows and front door out of curiosity. One night he slept on the porch of my next door neighbor, after she had watched him turning somersaults on her fence. My trail camera spied him sniffing logs, prancing through the woods with a youthful exuberance . So when bear hunting season began the first day of September, and we heard that a hunter driving down the highway had spotted a three-year old black bear crossing the road, then waited till he crossed and legally shot him, we hoped it wasn't 'our' little bear.

Bear hunters rarely eat their kill but hunt for trophy. Although I don't agree with trophy hunting, I was even more appalled at this hunter's ethics and clear lack of sportsmanship. Clearly, a young cub, no bigger than my golden retriever, just newly out on his own, was no trophy. We all waited to see if our little cub might reappear on my camera. When he did a week later, we rejoiced.

I tell this story only to illustrate the great ontological chasm between how we view bears now in contrast to our recent past. Are bears sentient beings? Or only objects, fodder for puffing up our sense of power and manliness? Throughout most of human history, we held these top predators in great esteem. They were the shamans of the animal world, magnificent and magical creatures who taught us what foods to eat and what medicinal plants to use. We dressed up like them and danced; we sought their spirit energy; we formed powerful secret societies of men and women who had 'bear guardians.' Many cultures considered bears sacred, not to be hunted. Some hunted bears for food. Yet to openly boast about the kill was dishonorable. The bear made a gift of its life and boasting of the kill denied that gift and violated the hunter's union with the animal's spirit. Bears were numinous beings, powerful, respected, honored, imitated. This is the spirit of approach we have forgotten. This is the orientation we must assume in order to protect these special animals. It is not just a matter of the Endangered Species Act. It is an act in consciousness that must occur.

We must be reborn again, into a new approach to living with the Great Bear. We are a richer species by just walking with grizzlies in these woods. To walk with the Great Bear one must be alert, fully awake and aware. All one's senses must be engaged. With the Great Bear around, you cannot walk lost in thought, or conversation. You must be Present. This alone is a gift that only another top predator can bring to man. The grizzly bear's gift to man is the Power of the Present Moment. The Present is his present to us. He presses it upon us by circumstance. Men do not give themselves that gift by choice. That is the gift of the grizzly.

"A person's life is not a series of dramatic events for which he or she is applauded or exiled but a slow accumulation of days, seasons, years, fleshed out by the generational weight of one's family and anchored by a land-bound sense of place."

Gretel Ehrlich

CHAPTER 8

Sagebrush Stories

Wyoming is the Land of Story. Once I began to spend more time here and meet people, I quickly found Wyomingites loved to relate their thoughts and feelings through story. Whether in business or pleasure, every interaction is a 'visit'. There are stories of breaking horses, of rodeo riding, of guiding and ranching. Of the time the mountain lightning was so intense it caused little sparks to rise on their fingers while holding the reins. And of the forty-seven-inch trout caught ice fishing in '62 down at New Fork Lakes. Of the nine cords of wood "I tried to sell 'em cheap" with the house, but that fellow said, "I'm putting in electric heat," and then it got 30 below in Pinedale, the electricity went off, and he had to haul his whole family to a motel in town. Those are the abbreviated versions. The embellished ones keep you captive.

People here read the weather by the movement of the deer or the seasonal shifts of the birds. They remember a year by the large population of ground squirrels or an overwhelming plague of grasshoppers. Time is punctuated by rare sightings — of a wolf making a kill, a mountain lion stalking a deer, a buffalo skull found by the river. The intense quiet and overwhelming geography make long gaps in a conversation comfortable, even necessary. I stop to say hello to a neighbor. Standing in the dirt driveway by the fenced meadow, large cumulus clouds pass over. The sky turns brilliant colors as the day comes to a close. We pause to watch. There is a rightness to it, as if in church — here, we are in church. It is the Land.

Sensitive, tender feelings that are rarely exposed in the suburbs or cities are part of a visit's conversation. The Land requires it; the depth of what a person encounters every day in this vast landscape forces a direct confrontation with powerful emotions. The drama of life and death going on continuously in the natural world contextualizes one's feelings. And the land itself, so dry and raw, wears its scars boldly, weathered bit by bit. Centuries of wounds appear etched on her face — trapper cabins, old 50's uranium scraps, horse skulls announcing past bear bait sites, mining shafts, Indian remains. It is as if the tender feelings exposed here are reflected on the Lands wrinkly surfaces. The immense space implies an endlessness of time. And here in Wyoming, time is what people do have.

* * * * * *

During the first spring at the cabin I met my neighbor Jack. One morning I looked out my front picture window and saw an old man with a rifle in his hand, walking across my lawn. Whoa, this just doesn't happen in California! Since I didn't own a gun, I walked out as confidently as I could and introduced myself.

"I'm on the easement to the Forest," he said. "See these lilacs? I planted them for Doc Firor where the easement starts. I'm gonna check on my spring. You know, there're bears and wolves out there.

Gotta carry a gun."

Jack and I shared water rights on one of my two springs. In Wyoming, it's always good to discuss water with one's neighbor. Along with his wife Jane, we quickly became fast friends. And Jack was the real deal. Born in the valley, raised in the valley, schooled at the one-room schoolhouse in the valley, his very blood flowed with the green shoots and clear waters of the basin. Jack's grandfather came to Cody sometime in the 1890s. His granddad was a guide for Buffalo Bill and owned a livery barn in town. Sometime in the early 1900s, Jack's father took out a homestead claim in these mountains. His homestead is in a unique and beautiful hollow below the main road. From this hidden depression, you can look out over the meadow, where their horses graze, and view the huge prominence of Bald Ridge, the wind-swept expanse of meadows at over eight thousand feet high above. He told me how he'd once walked to town, forty-five miles away, over the pass. It took him all day. No one does that these days.

During my first visits with Jack and Jane, we talked mostly about two things: water and that I should carry a gun. Most every conversation turned back to water rights in Wyoming and to our little spring, and ended with "I shouldn't be hiking without a gun in this country." It would have been futile to discuss the merits of bear spray over a gun.

When my first summer rolled around, Jack gave me good advice. "It's easy to get rim-rocked around here. If you do, just follow the game trails, they'll take you downhill the easiest way."

"What's rim-rocked?" I asked. I'd never heard that expression before.

"You're trying to get downhill and instead you're at a cliff with no way out" was his reply. I'd soon find that happens frequently around here.

I reveled in Jack's stories. At eighty-four he was losing his hearing, but certainly not his mind, which was sharper than mine on most days. He could remember dates and names, years of winter storms and the rhythms of game through the various seasons.

Whenever my son, Michael, came for a stay I always liked to take him for a visit with Jack and Jane. On one occasion we traipsed over to their small trailer; it was a day after we had been hiking to Copper lakes at the head of the valley. Our hike came up in conversation.

"Are those cabins still up there?" Jack asked. When we said no, he replied, "Last time I was there was in '47." I think my twenty-year-old son's jaw just about fell out.

Jack had stories from the early days of his childhood on the homestead, his adult life working in the Park, his years of developing water for the ranchers in Pinedale, and his time as a deputy sheriff in the valley. He had me at 'go!'

Probably more than anybody, Jack spurred my curiosity to learn about the history of the valley. Sometimes he'd tell me a tale about a particular area, then I'd hike to try to find it. Lots of times it was the other way around. Through him, a whole new world opened up — the world of 'the way it was,' a hundred years before.

One day Jack said, 'Wanna go for a ride?'

And of course I readily took him up on it. We rode his horses to the nearby Elk Creek drainage. I'd hiked the wide drainage many times, but this time Jack turned into a rough and arduous side canyon.

"This is my secret spot. Don't tell anyone about it." We rode to a fork in the narrow canyon. Sheer impressive bluffs hovered above. Jack continued along the right fork, following a small seep thick with young aspens. Veering upslope, we passed through a lightly wooded area of douglas firs and limber pines. The horses strained with the incline until finally we came to a clearing at the top of the mountain. We dismounted and I looked around.

"I've slept here many times. This is the place."

I could see the entire valley. From that vantage, I asked about some small lakes I'd tried to find, or an old cabin I'd searched for. He pointed out features in the landscape, attempting to visually guide me through the route. Before we had lunch, I told him to stand by his horse while I snapped a picture. I had a feeling this might be the last time he made it here. A few birthdays later I gave him the photo.

We ate and admired the country, then set off for home by a different route. There was no trail. Jack followed along the hogback,

Before we had lunch, I told him to stand by his horse while I snapped a picture.

searching for a game trail to cross back over into our valley. We descended by a precipitous, wooded game trail, crowded with pencil-thin pines. The trail became so abrupt that we had to walk the horses. Jack's knees were hurting. We sat and rested half way down and I asked Jack to finish the story he once told me about his grandfather.

"My grandfather was born in Nebraska. When he was just nine years old, he was playing and broke his leg. His father was a hard man and beat him for that. My grandpa swore to himself that when he got better he was going to run away and he did, at ten years old. He and a friend were catching rides on freighters going down river, going West. They hitched a ride on a wagon that was attacked by Indians. The Indians killed everyone in that wagon train, including his friend, but my grandpa hid in a flour drum.

"The Chief and his wife found my grandfather and the Chief's wife took pity on him. They took him back to the tribe and raised him with their own child, which I think was a girl. That Chief was Standing Bear. My Grandpa lived with them for five years.

"Indians like to gamble and compete. There was one boy the same age as my grandfather who didn't get along with him at all. When my grandpa was fifteen, this boy challenged my grandfather to a horse race. Grandfather was an excellent horseman and he was winning. The Indian boy was mad and pulled out a knife. Grandpa knocked that boy down, off his horse, and I think he killed him. Or hurt him badly. No, I think he killed him, but it was kill or be killed.

"The whole tribe had a meeting. Since my grandfather was white, they banished him. Chief Standing Bear and his wife took my grandpa in the middle of the night, on horseback, and told him he should leave and go far away; far enough away so no one in the tribe would come after him. The Chief told him that he would always love him and think of him as a son, strong, brave and worthy to become a chief, but that now he must go. Grandpa came out to this country and spent time here with the Shoshone as well. He was taking people on pack trips into the Park when Buffalo Bill came out here.

"It's true he had a wooden leg. He was logging and in an accident. His leg broke, a clean break right here (points to below his knee). He knew how to set bones and had set many breaks on other people. But they took him to a doctor who cut off his leg at the knee. That shouldn't have been. He'd wear lots and lots of socks over that peg to cushion it against his knee. But he could do anything he wanted with that leg.

"He lived near the mouth of the Clark's Fork. One time us kids were down there visiting. My sister was taking a nap in the house and all of us other kids were down at the river swimming and fishing. Grandpa was working in his shop nearby. In those days there was lots of sheet lightening in this country. My sister had just gotten up from her nap and was coming down to the river, when lightening struck the house. You couldn't do nothing. In an instant, the entire house was in flames. My grandpa thought my little sister was still in the house. You should've seen him run with that peg leg!"

One beautiful fall day I helped Jack saddle up the horses for a ride. He led me along the river, across the highway, and down to his family's homestead. He doesn't stay there anymore, but still has a tiny cabin. He unbolted the front door. The entire cabin was not much bigger than my living room. An old Majestic wood cook stove sat directly across from the front door, used for heat and cooking. After he'd opened up the curtains, he showed me the bedroom. The room was barely big enough for a log double bed built by his son. I noticed a small branch on the wall and asked Jack about it.

"Why, that's part of the tree I was born under on Dead Indian hill. My mother was in a wagon, trying to get to town. She never made it. I was born on the mountain under a pine tree."

All I could think about was *I want to have been born under a tree!*

I'd heard lots of stories about Dead Indian Pass: how treacherous it used to be; how once you were here in the winter, you stayed in the valley for the winter as the hill was impassable, deep in snow and drifts; and about the old ax-cut logs at the bottom of Dead Indian hill, left from the earliest days of travel across the mountain.

When a wagon reached the top of the pass, they'd stop and cut some trees. Then they'd chain them to the wagon axle, limbs and all, to provide some drag. That way the wagon wouldn't overtake the horses, and run away. There's a story about one fifteen-year-old boy who was all alone, leading a horse-drawn wagon over the pass. When he got to the top, he felled several trees and tied them to the axles. But he didn't tie enough weight, and once on the slopes, the wagon began to catch up with the horses. He whipped those horses as fast as they could go till he made it safe at the bottom. They say, "He was a boy at the top, but a man when he got to the bottom."

The 'road' at that time was just an old Indian pony and game trail. The most treacherous section was called the 'beaver slide.' At the bottom of the slide was where the men unhooked the logs from the wagons.

The road's gone through about four improvements since its Indian trail days. The timeline was still sketchy for me as to all the road improvements, but I understood that around 1905 some of the residents living in the valley asked the county for assistance to improve the road. The money was approved; a passable upgrade, an actual dirt road instead of a trail, was built — mostly by the residents in the valley. The Painter Ranch, one of the original homesteaders, pitched in with a four-horse team, a breaking plow, and one man, while Al Beam, another of the first residents did the same. Miners who had claims in the valley helped blast rocks. By 1909 the new grade was completed, with a series of switchbacks. This was essentially the dirt road used for the next eighty years until the early 1990s. A fully paved road completed in 1993 marked the end of quiet isolation and the beginning of traffic and visitors the valley had never before seen. Jack told me that he now sees more cars in one day than, in the past, he saw all year.

I wanted to walk the original dirt road; it's easy to find. It's still in fair condition. But the trail is a lot more difficult. It's been over one hundred years since it was used. A good game trail still runs through the creek drainage and you can see a semblance of the original pony trail following it. I understood from reading old texts that this game trail had arrowheads and Indian pony tracks all over it. The route had been used for thousands of years.

Walking alongside a narrow creek, a definite split occurs where the animal trail turns southwest up into another drainage. It's at this point the southerly route over Dead Indian hill changes course markedly and veers up a steep hillside. From this vantage I couldn't see where or even how a team of horses could go up it.

Above the trail and following a natural ridgeline, was the improved 1909 road. I detoured up the hillside and headed towards it. I wanted to walk that too. I'd lost any evidence of the original game trail. The road, cut by hand and horse, was a marvel to look at. Although it had been improved over the years to accommodate cars, it still possessed its original character. The final paved road up the mountain detours greatly from this dirt route since it employs generous switchbacks.

With the car and truck traffic now utilizing other areas of the mountain, wildlife take advantage of the dirt road and its cover. It skirts the highway enough so they are hidden and in at least one area a spring emerges alongside the road cut. Hundreds of winter elk and deer tracks criss-crossed over the wet mud. I rounded a corner and found a cow elk winter kill.

The dirt road petered out in a large meadow. A Forest Service fence line and livestock trough marked a cattle allotment. I headed back down, keeping an eye out for where a wagon might have veered off. Pretty soon, I came to a gently sloping meadow and followed it, leaving the dirt byway. The meadow gave way to sharp wooded incline. It was at this spot that I saw a series of young trees the width of a wagon. Old ruts were faintly visible. This had to be 'the beaver slide,' the place where the slope was most precarious.

I hiked down noticing the grade was quite sheer and treacherous for a wagon. At the bottom of the slide, a clearing opened above a fork in a dry stream. This was the fork I had missed earlier, where the drainage split. Lots of old dead trees were scattered around the open area. I wouldn't say they were piled, but upon closer inspection you could see they'd been ax cut. Here it was, the logs that had been cut by those old timers to prevent run-away wagons.

The history of this place was palpable: the cut logs holding back the wagons from tumbling down the hillside; the herculean efforts of these men to build a better and safer road with only man and horse power; the old trail used for thousands of years by Indians on foot and later with their ponies. Though I was the only one walking these trails today, the stories and ghosts of the past walked beside me.

* * * * * *

Jane told me that as late as the 1970s "they plowed the road when they needed to. Like when they wanted to get equipment or supplies up here for something. We watched the weather and waited for the plow if we wanted to go to town. Most of the time we just planned on staying here without going to town all winter. That was when the road was dirt."

The pass is infamous amongst old-timers and everyone has their favorite story. One resident recalled Art Holman, the fellow who carried the mail into the valley.

In bad weather Art loaded one of his horses in the back of his four-wheel Dodge Power Wagon. Sometimes, when forced to abandon his vehicle, he hitched his horse to a sleigh that he had cached near the divide...We heard of times when he took the truck as far as it would go, then the sleigh until that got stuck, then continued on horseback, and finally tied his exhausted horse and finished the route on skis.

Back in the 1930s, Jack and some men snowshoed a forest ranger with appendicitis over the pass. Taking turns, they pulled the sick man in the sled thirty-five miles into town. Although it took them all day, "he lived," Jack said.

Residents still talk about 'fighting the mountain' in the winter. I fight it once a week when I go for supplies and to volunteer at the local museum. I've had more than a few hairy moments, like the evening in October when I was in town for a movie on Aldo Leopold. October can be gorgeous weather, but also unpredictable. I left the movie theater after dark, around 8:30 p.m. The moon was bright and the sky was clear. I approached the base of the mountain;

low clouds were moving in fast. As I climbed the switchbacks, the weather worsened. The snow was coming down heavy and the fog was so dense, I was inside the clouds. Rising higher and higher, the fog grew impenetrable. By the time I reached the pass, I could no longer see the road at all. I stopped at the top of the pass and pondered my predicament. Here the road, downhill, winds through tortuous curves with a sheer cliff on one side. If I couldn't see the road nor see ahead of me for all the heavy snow, what should I do? I decided that sleeping on the top of the pass was not a good thing, so I rolled down the window and drove through the clouds with my head outside in the snow, straining to see where the guard rail was. Of course, my trials with the mountain are laughable to old-timers here.

Allie Ritterbrown, an early resident in the valley, describes a harrowing event on the wintery slopes of Dead Indian in the 1930s. I'd heard a lot of stories about her from Jack and from others. In a partial manuscript given to me, she describes driving over the mountain in a 1928 Buick touring car. The car had no windows and it was in the days before windshield wipers. Before Allie and her husband started the trip they put chains on the tires, then pulled the car battery out from the basement, a common practice in winter. With no wipers, they carried a bag of salt and a putty knife to clear the ice. In case they broke down, they brought some jerky, a buffalo robe, a bedroll, two shovels and a lantern. As the journey began up the treacherous north-facing slope, they hit the first big drift and shoveled themselves out. And proceeded on to the next drift and the next, until a Game and Fish pickup came around a switchback above them. The government truck had spooked an elk herd that was running at full speed. Allie's first thought was how much easier it will be going uphill since the Game truck had shoveled the drifts and made tracks upon their descent. But she soon realized that even when the road was dry it was only a single-track road. Now how was the Game truck going to pass beside them without any road to spare?

The men shoveled the snow from the edge of the cliff over to the steep bank. They then drove the Buick into the uphill side so it was leaning against the trees, got out ropes and tied the car to hold it from tipping over. The Game Warden was driving slowly, almost falling off the slope, while the other men held the truck by the ropes. After the Game Warden passed, the men attended to the Buick in the ditch using poles and jacks to get it on its four wheels again. The Warden got out a bottle of bourbon and offered it around.

* * * * * *

I have an early map of all the homesteads and mining claims in the valley. Official homestead claims start around 1915. Mine was listed as 'Ellsbury.' I was always asking Jack if he knew this person or that person, what was their story, what was the land like then.

"In those days, people were always coming through this country on horseback. I'd come home and never know who might be there. The first thing you'd ask is "have you had supper?" and the traveler would stay for a night, usually on his bedroll on the floor, after eating a meal, feeding his horse, chopping some wood; he'd be on his way in the morning. Then you might not see him again for a year.

"I remember one old timer who came around sometimes when I was a kid. I'd ask him 'when did you first come to this country?' And this old timer would always say 'when I got here the mountains were flat.'" Jack would tell me that story, then laugh and laugh.

There were two old schoolhouses, in different locations, in the valley. One was a two-room building with dilapidated furniture. Jack said this was the original schoolhouse built by the very earliest homesteaders at the turn of the century. The other, the updated one, was a small cabin that sat near the valley's mouth.

"I went there from first through sixth grade. We had the first schoolteacher in the basin. She was a young and pretty lady and of course all the cowboys up here were interested. She liked to hike, so lots of time she'd take all of us kids for a morning hike around Steamboat ridge."

When Jack was growing up, it had only been less than fifty years since Indians were roaming through these lands. In a draw named Tipi Gulch in the valley, Jack said there were teepees up on the ridgeline. But he hasn't been up there in years and no teepee rings are visible anymore. But he'd found lots of Indian sign around — lookouts and picture writings.

"I once found a place where they'd set up smoke signals. Hidden under a rock were some beads. I just kept them there and I'm not telling anyone where that is. This one's gonna die with me. Every time I tell someone about something I find, they go and dig it up and take it away for themselves."

I'd heard about a box canyon along one of the creeks that had been an overwintering campsite for Indians for thousands of years. I also understood there was an old trapper's cabin there.

I had some crude instructions on how to find the place and immediately grabbed my map to figure where it might be. The hike was an easy one along the flats of the Clark's Fork plateau. The trail turns south into a narrow gully, rimmed by numerous ledges of stairstep boulders. After a short time, the creek appears. An impassable wall of boulders downstream blocks further travel. But upstream lies a small meadow providing good camping creekside. The water was low enough in August that I could rock hop the river. Just across the other side was the old cabin. The cabin no longer had a roof and couldn't have been bigger than a child's bedroom. It was hard for me to imagine a person actually living year here round, but a man named Thompson did. A dug out area at the back of the cabin was where the root cellar had been, now filled with trash from kids spending the night. In a sunny area stood a large pile of small rocks. Thompson had cleared a patch in order to grow some vegetables, probably mostly potatoes.

"So you found ol' man Thompson's cabin. " Jack said. After the hike I asked him about the cabin's owner. "My grandpa knew Thompson. Sometimes he'd go over there for a visit. One time he had dinner there, and when they were cleaning up and doing the dishes, Thompson blew his nose in the dishrag and kept wiping

"So you found ol' man Thompson's cabin."

the dishes with it. That was the last time he had dinner with the man. Thompson was a trapper, you know. He also grew a few vegetables. He'd take his produce by wagon up to Cooke City and sell them in the summer. In the winter, he'd trap, and in the fall he'd take all his pelts to Cody and trade them for staples, like flour and sugar. And he had a still and made liquor. He'd take that to town too. He had stills all over the place, hidden."

I'd spied a place past the Thompson's cabin where two enormous house-size granitic boulders form a narrow tunnel. Ground water runs through the slot, which is thick with vegetation — dogwoods, roses, and berries. I'd been waiting all summer for the water to dry up some so I could slip through this secret passageway. I thought it might be a quick way to the river.

The ground was muddy but the water wasn't running and the bugs were gone after an early frost. I'd inspected the area from the cliffs above and could see the walled tunnel was around a hundred feet in length. I approached the massive rock wall entrance, only about three-feet wide, and the first thing I saw was a grizzly print. I was certain few people had gone through this passageway or even knew about it, but the animals sure used it. I didn't want to meet a bear coming at me on my way into the tunnel. With my bear spray in hand, I pushed aside brush and made my way along the narrow rock corridor. The passage had an Alice in Wonderland effect, as if I was going down the hole. I emerged into a completely different world, just a few feet above the river. A beautiful cave seep was to my right. In front of me was a shelter of some sort constructed crudely of very old logs. It had the look of a wikiup fallen apart with age or possibly an old Indian corral used creekside for ponies.

I crossed the river, which is low at this time of year and made my way into a wooded canyon. The bear had been spending time here looking for pine nuts. His scat was everywhere. As I explored the canyon, I found it was 'T' shaped. At the junction, canyon walls climbed a few hundred feet to a wind-swept plateau above. But down below, it was a protected and hidden cavity. I discovered a wide and deep mound, covered intentionally, apparently, with old logs and debris — a cache maybe? Jack had said that Old Man Thompson had caches and stills hidden everywhere. I turned at the junction and made my way through open woods. I could see light ahead. The trees abated and I stood on a slope almost directly above and across the river from Thompson's cabin. Here was another, elusive entrance to these unusual woods amidst the open rocky flats. Thompson knew about this area. I'm sure he used to make his whiskey here being so well hidden. Jack wasn't familiar with the boulder passageway.

"What happened to Thompson?" I asked him.

"I don't know. I think he just up and left one day." He chuckled and said "Maybe this country just got too crowded for him."

* * * * * *

While visiting Jack and Jane at their home in town, I noticed a photograph on the coffee table. The picture had been taken close to the homestead — I could tell from the environs. Centered in the photo was a large rectangular wooden box without a lid. The box butted up against the side of a large boulder, wedged between several other large rocks. A pile of smaller rocks sat to the side. There was no bottom to the box and some old bones were inside that looked like an elk pelvis. I asked Jack about it.

"Why that's where old Frank Hammitt's body was buried, in a wagon box. They covered the box and put rocks over the top. You can still see the wood down there if you can find it."

I knew about Frank Hammitt. He was one of the first six forest rangers appointed in the United States. The Shoshone National Forest was the first National Forest in the country, signed into law in 1891. A plaque for Hammitt, who died at the age of thirty-four in 1903, having been a ranger since 1898, stands at the base of Antelope Butte. Antelope Butte is an amazing formation, right out of a western movie. Perfectly flat on top with three vertical sides, it's accessible only from the north, which is now on private land.

Frank Hammitt lore abounds. Some tales say he committed suicide by jumping off the side of the butte. Others claim it was a very foggy night, Frank was riding his horse on the top of the butte, and he didn't see the ledge. Both the horse and Frank fell to their deaths. Another version is that he was drunk and fell off Antelope Butte in the middle of a winter night. Jack was about to retell me the tale, and I knew it would be the honest truth.

"My grandpa and dad knew Frank. They found his horse wandering around. Whenever you see someone's horse, you know you better start looking for its rider. They found Frank over the cliff, way down on a ledge, on the Russell Creek side near the canyon's edge. There was a pile of smoked cigarettes on a rock nearby. Hard to say what happened. No one knows. He was pretty ripe. Been there a while. Pretty ripe. It must have taken quite a few men and ropes to haul him back up."

The canyon cliffs Jack was talking about were at least two miles from Antelope Butte. In Jack's version, Frank fell into the Clark's Fork drainage, not over the Butte.

"I was young then and my dad used to say to us, 'You boys just stay away from that box. Don't git near there.' After some time, a fellow living on the other side of the road, well, he decided that

Frank needed a more proper burial. So he took his wagon down there, collected Frank's bones. And you know, he didn't get them all. There're still some bones in there. But he collected some of them and brought them up by wagon to the place where the memorial is now. He buried the bones there, stuck two posts in the ground.

"That was around 1938 (*35 years after Hammitt's death*). The CCC (*Civilian Conservation Corps*) built that memorial that's there now. Folks will tell all sorts of stories: they like to talk about Frank dying by falling off the butte. But that's just not what happened, and here's the picture to prove it."

Jack's story fired me up — another historical mystery to explore. That area is full of rocks and arroyos and covers a lot of ground. Without Jack taking me to the makeshift coffin, it would be hard to find.

They found Frank over the cliff, way down on a ledge.

The following winter I was tooling around on the flats when I ran smack into the coffin. It was just as the photo showed, up against a beautiful boulder fairly close to the treacherous edge of the canyon. I assumed I was near the spot where Frank fell to his death. I walked over to the canyon's edge and looked over the rim. It's a bumpy thousand-foot drop to the canyon bottom. I imaged them hauling him up, finding this nearby beautiful boulder for a tombstone, and placing his decomposing body in a wagon box. The lid was now gone, but I could still see the smaller rocks that they'd placed on top of the lid. Some old elk bones were lying in and around the box, but I sure didn't see any of old Frank's bones there. But of course, its' been over a hundred years since he died.

* * * * * *

Besides the Buick incident, I'd learned quickly that Allie Ritterbrown was a legend in my valley. When I arrived, she had died several years earlier in Berkeley, California, where she spent her later years. All that was left of her large ranch that once took in most of the land at the mouth of the basin was an eleven-acre parcel belonging to her kids. Several years later, that piece was sold off as well, the end of an era, yet her colorful influence is still felt.

Allie herself was a transplant from back East. She was an educated city dweller who fell in love with a Cody local and came to Wyoming in the 1930s to live on her husband's ranch. The first shock of her new life must have come with that two-day trip over Dead Indian pass. It was a hard life in the 1930s for Allie up here. No electricity, no running water, she had to learn to cook on a Majestic wood stove, wrangle horses, grow hay, and negotiate the harrowing road over the mountain a few times a year for supplies. A feisty woman with an artistic eye, she was better at drawing people to the ranch than at managing it. When they decided to run it as a dude outfit, she probably was already in debt, because slowly over time she traded or sold off pieces of her property to the wealthy New England 'dudes' to pay the bills. Many of them, who came yearly to her ranch, were inspired to buy land or move here through their association with Allie.

When Allie arrived from New York in December 1934, she experienced quite a culture shock. She'd never ridden a horse let alone lived out in the hinterlands of the mountains where all winter was passed without access to town. She wrote:

People in the country seldom ran out of anything. They got in such an order of staples in the fall that the root cellar and pantry looked like a grocery store. I had never seen anything like it — a half a ton of flour, five hundred pounds of sugar, one hundred pounds of coffee, and a root cellar full of all the garden stuff that could be kept over the winter, like potatoes, carrots and celery in a trough of white sand to keep bleached, as well as hundreds and hundreds of jars of vegetables from the garden, jam made of wild gooseberries and chokecherries and serviceberries, pickles and relish and everything imaginable. I realized when I saw all this that someone had worked long and hard. I began to appreciate every jar that I opened.

I began to learn to cook on a wood stove. My main trouble was that I didn't yet know how much wood to put in the stove. If I got too much in and didn't adjust the dampers just right, the cake burned to a crisp in five minutes. So the next time I put green wood in and closed the dampers and an hour and a half later the gingerbread was still liquid in the middle, the fire was out, and I was almost in tears.

One classic story about Allie told me a lot about her as a person and a fighter for justice. During the second World War, over

11,000 Japanese-Americans were interned in a camp at the base of Heart Mountain, a prominent landmark above Cody. The stores in town refused to serve Japanese-Americans and there were other mistreatments as well.

Allie abhorred this discrimination and she had an idea how to fight it. She went to the internment camp and talked with the commander, asking him to call a meeting of all the internees. Once gathered, the commander announced, "This lady is willing to make all the stores that are refusing you service remove their signs."

Allie asked those assembled to give her a list of people willing to run for office in the next local election. The crowd started to laugh when they understood what she was going to do. The commander later told her this was the first time he'd ever heard them laugh. With her list of volunteers, she went before the local meeting of merchants and politicians, all of them men.

"There are more voters and people of voting age out at Heart Mountain than there are in this whole county. If you don't start treating them like human beings, I'm going out there and I'll register them all to vote. And you'll have a Japanese mayor and a Japanese courthouse, and all the rest." The signs came down and the stores began serving Japanese-Americans.

* * * * * *

As a newcomer, I've barely scratched the surface of stories waiting to be told to me around campfires, at the dinner table with friends, or on hikes in these mountains. Old-timers have many more vivid stories than I've even begun here. But that is what makes these places and people so special, and forever interesting.

"A quarter of a mile away, six coyotes disappeared single-file into the forest. I thought, How amazing that there are so many coyotes around. Yet we hardly ever see coyotes, even though their wildness is among us. It is everywhere, but it is hidden and secret. Most of us don't know much about the world of coyotes, but coyotes know a lot about ours. They watch and listen to us."

Paul Rezendes

CHAPTER 9

Medicine Dog

One fall afternoon after a hike, I was at the small local campground, retrieving my car, where I met a couple lounging in front of their travel trailer. He'd worked as a driller, had operated heavy equipment, grew up in Wyoming, and lived and worked most of his life in the backcountry. She'd been coming to this area to camp since childhood.

"Pack a good gun when you hike on account of bears. I'd never hike up there without a gun," he said, pointing in the direction from where I had just arrived. He sounded like Jack. "And also those caves up there are dangerous because the air is dead in the back of them and you'll suffocate and not even know it." He had lots of advice, most of which I was already not following.

As we chatted about the area he told me an interesting story about raising a coyote: a friend of his had killed the mother coyote with three pups. The other men were taking pups so he took one.

"They say you can't raise a coyote, but I did. I also had a German Shepherd who was a year and a half. That shepherd kept the coyote in its place for over a year. The coyote used to disappear for days or a week at a time. Other coyotes would come around and howl, trying to entice the baby to join them, and sometimes she would. But she'd come back. It was four years before I could pet that coyote. She used to sleep against my leg, but wouldn't let me touch her. Finally after four years I could pet the coyote, and when she was older I could love it. Smarter than any dog.

"There was a Game & Fish warden who was my boss on a project I was working on. I was making a road. He'd come up there and we'd talk across in our trucks. I didn't like this man. He was always down on the work I was doing, which was good work. And the coyote didn't like him either. We'd be talking and when we'd finish… you know how you have your arm laying on the window…well, he'd have his arm out as he drove away. The coyote, you know she was in the back of my truck, would nip at his hand when we'd pass, every time. And she didn't do that to no one else. So that warden started keeping his arms inside. One day I was working way up on the mountain and here comes the warden. I don't know how that coyote recognized him, but she did and she started chasing him down the mountain. The warden ran down and into his truck and got away as fast as he could. There was something wrong with that man and the coyote sensed it."

It's a strange thing how we've turned coyotes on their heads, completely opposite to how they were treated before the white man came here. Coyote is a predominate character in Native American stories. Coyote is both trickster and hero. I think most people are familiar with coyote Indian stories, yet their meanings are much harder to grasp. Of course, we don't really know coyotes anymore, we don't observe them in their natural setting and in play with other animals, and we ourselves don't live in a world from which these stories sprang.

Coyote stories can't be neatly divided into hero stories and trickster stories. He is hero/trickster and must be taken as facets of the same character. Barry Lopez states: *The dichotomy itself is an artificial one, a creation of the Western mind, but a forceful one.*

Coyote as hero brings important things into this world, such as the animals, or humans, or gives fire to humans.

And coyote the trickster? That is harder to define. Paul Radin in *The Trickster* summarizes the coyote this way:

"Trickster is at one and the same time creator and destroyer, giver and negator, he who dupes others and who is always duped himself. . . . He possesses no values, moral or social, is at the mercy of his passions and appetites, yet through his actions all values come into being"

Coyotes are bold, display hubris, yet are also cunning, patient, and furtive. I've watched them hunt by sneaking patiently, step-by-step, listening and waiting for ground squirrels to emerge from

Coyote hunting for voles

their holes. But I've also seen them weave in and out of an elk herd looking for a possible meal, only to be kicked in the ribs and die. One day I saw a feisty coyote being chased one-quarter of a mile over several hillocks by two Angus cows. The cows were relentless, close on the heels of the coyote. Finally when they reached the pasture's fence line, the coyote slipped underneath the wire, escaping from the angry cows. And what did the coyote do? He immediately peed in defiance on the nearest sagebrush from the other side of the fence, as if to say 'Ha, ha, That was fun and you can't catch me!"

Another time in Yellowstone I observed a coyote nonchalantly zigzagging through sagebrush, slowly approaching a small group of five cow bison with a newborn calf. What was the coyote thinking, I wondered, as he can't take on bison? The coyote approached indirectly through the tall brush. The bison encircled the calf. The coyote boldly advanced within just a stone's throw. I expected the bison to charge. But instead, as the coyote moved in, the bison cows sandwiched the calf between them, one bison facing one direction with the other facing opposite, squeezing the calf invisibly in the center. The coyote knew his jig was up and headed for another possible meal.

Every culture has their trickster. The trickster is the embodiment of opposites, of extremes. He makes you laugh at the absurd, or at his foibles. Jung described the trickster as the *shadow side of a culture* — all the things that are hidden the trickster presents out in the open and that dark energy is expressed and released through story. No matter how much you read about the trickster, he is enigmatic and cannot be grasped by the mind. Coyotes themselves have many facets to their personality: they can hunt independently or in packs, they can ally with other animals for a meal, they can feed up and down the food chain. The coyote as trickster reminds me of the Tibetan Crazy Wisdom tradition. The tradition of Crazy Wisdom tells of Enlightened Masters who taught through living paradox: their life and teachings (and some had no teachings at all) were expressions of unconditional freedom. They lived lives outside the conventional agreements of morality, religion and social contracts. Their very existence in Time and Space exploded and confounded our assumption that we are living as limited mortal beings. They were unpredictable, unorthodox, breaking all taboos. Not one Master was alike. Some acted just as you might expect a spiritual teacher to act; but others might spend their lives living on a pile of dung, or drinking wine and having lots of sex. The only thing they all had in common was their commitment to the 'undoing' of anyone whom they came into contact with; the undoing of the ego and the awakening of the individual to his or her transcendental Self. The tradition of Crazy Wisdom was taught through paradox and contradiction.

Coyote, as creator and destroyer, rogue, knave, fool, playboy, god, seducer, giver of fire and death to humans, is the crazy adept of American Indian cultures. Coyote stories are funny and silly yet profound and sacred at the same time. There is a depth that is untouchable and indescribable. Here is one coyote story in brief:

Coyote the Trickster comes upon a flock of ducks by a lake. He tricks them into dancing with their eyes closed. During the dance he kills most of them, then sets them to roasting over a fire. While they cook, he goes to sleep after appointing his anus to guard the meat. When a group of foxes chances upon the scene, the anus attempts to drive them off by flatulating, but to no avail. The foxes eat all the ducks. When Trickster awakens, he is so angry with his anus that he burns it with a brand from the fire. Then, as he walks along, he sees pieces of cooked fat on the trail, which he eats. He discovers, much to his surprise, that these pieces of meat are fragments of his own burned intestines.

Coyote is a totem and in choosing him as their culture hero and trickster, native peoples have bestowed a great honor as well as power to this creature. Coyote is given the power to stop the mind just as the Zen Master's stick gives the blow of Enlightenment to his student. Coyote frees us from stodgy mind, lightens the spirit, and creates an opening for creativity and inspiration. Trickster Coyote is essential for contact with the sacred. Many native traditions held that people cannot pray until they have laughed, for laughter opens and frees us from rigidity and preconceptions. And least we humans forget, the sacred comes through surprise, upset, difficulty.

Coyote in his multiplicity of forms, unlike European clown-type tricksters, acknowledges our own dualistic nature — Yin and Yang, Good and Evil, Form and Formless. In the embrace of Paradox, we are Free. Coyote is here to guide us by virtue of his Crazy Wisdom — his Tricksterness — beyond Time and Space.

One morning in Yellowstone I saw a crowd of cars stopped in the middle of the road; people had gotten out their binoculars and scopes. I asked what they were observing. One woman answered, "A coyote is stalking a badger." I knew immediately that the coyote and the badger were hunting together, albeit an uneasy partnership. I watched the two animals for a while. The badger was actively searching out holes with the coyote resting nearby. After a while, the coyote began stalking again, slinking and listening for ground squirrels.

American Indians had long observed these two species' hunting partnership and told many stories about it; but amazingly it wasn't until 1992 that a study in California confirmed this coordinated hunting technique. Coyotes, the biologists noted, caught a third more prey hunting with badgers.

I wonder if, once again, it's the coyote who is benefiting more from this relationship. Badgers and coyotes eat the same prey — burrowing animals — and when badgers dig for them, sometimes a squirrel bursts from the hole or out another exit, escaping from the badger and into the mouth of the waiting coyote. On the other hand, a coyote might miss his opportunity to catch a squirrel, which runs into his hole. The badger then digs it out.

The Chinooks used to tell this humorous story of the coyote and badger:

Coyote and Badger are again hunting, though along the river this time, and they are enjoying considerable success. In fact, their success is so great that other animals start to fear them and refuse to cooperate; they enter into a dry period. For a few days, they take up the previous weapons and seek game away from the river. Badger has continuing success but Coyote is a poor hunter.

The secret behind all of this is that Badger kills game with his farts. (Badgers have strong scent glands.) *So when Coyote finally recognizes this, he proposes that they trade assholes, and they do. Needless to say, lacking the crucial glands, poor Coyote finds Badger's asshole quite useless and, in frustration, he asks to trade back. So Badger secures his own from Coyote first and then throws Coyote's asshole in the river. Poor Coyote winds up tearing along the river, ripped by brush, watching young boys trying to hit his floating asshole with spears. When he finally recovers it, it is a mess; and Coyote whimpers off, the loser once more.*

* * * * * *

Coyotes are among the oldest indigenous species in North America, some three million years old. Their arch-enemy is the wolf. After the wolves were eradicated by the 1930s in the GYE, the coyotes became the bane of the sheep, cattle, chicken, and any other type of rancher. Coyotes were blamed for all troubles. With the reintroduction of wolves, however, 'coyote-blame' has taken a back-seat to wolves. Coyotes do some ranching damage, but prefer small game. Wolves, on the other hand, are fully equipped alone or in a pack, to take out large prey.

But if you want to naturally limit the coyote population within an ecological balance, you need the top predator in the ecosystem — wolves. The coyote population has been reduced between 30 and 70% due in large part to wolves who came on the scene in Yellowstone in the 1990s. Dr. Robert Crabtree, founder, chief scientist and president of the Yellowstone Ecological Research Center and a leading expert on coyotes, notes that wolves "have provided a constant selection factor inflicting mortality, competition, and numerous other sub-lethal effects. Collectively, these intense selective pressures by wolves resulted in a species that exists in a relatively constant state of colonization with many specialized adaptations."

Over thousands of years of dealing with wolves, coyotes have become cunning and adaptable under stress. While the coyotes in Yellowstone mostly eat ground squirrels — it takes a few to make a good meal — when wolves kill large prey, coyotes can take advantage of the leftovers. So it pays for coyotes to stick around wolves, but not too close. This stress has produced powerful survival skills. It seems coyotes evolved to do better in a state of flux.

In our attempt to eradicate the coyote, we have created optimal conditions for this change. For starters, we killed off the coyotes' primary enemy. Then we cultivated fields, creating open spaces and niches for rodents. These fields we filled with nice plump easy prey, like sheep and chickens, to help coyotes feed their pups. And then by putting stress on coyotes through trapping and killing, we acted like wolves. Yet, with our eradication programs, we will never be able to keep coyotes in check the way wolves do.

Crabtree continues, "These demographic and behavioral adaptations [to wolves] are numerous and diverse and allow coyote populations to easily overcome the relatively mild effects of human control practices which are short-term and intermittent compared to sustained presence of wolves."

Coyotes on a wolf kill

Coyotes have gone from an animal of the West, to a ubiquitous presence across North America. Fossil evidence indicates that coyotes once lived across much of the North American continent during the Pleistocene, though when Lewis and Clark discovered them they were largely confined to prairie grasslands. While working in California, I went for an evening walk in December from my residence to nearby Muir Beach. This winter had been unseasonably warm and dry, and people were crowding to the beach every weekend. I'd gotten into the habit of walking down to the beach around 5 p.m. to give my dog a nice run. The beach was only a short downhill stroll no more than fifty steps. On one side of these wooden stairs was a lawn and an adjacent house on the same property; on the other side was native brush, which was too congested to see into.

Dusk was settling in as Koda and I began our evening trek down the stairs. Suddenly, he ran off into the bushes. I called him back, then decided to go and explore. A compost pile sat in the thicket clearing. Just as I peered through, a large coy-dog ran off. Coy-dogs are dog/coyote hybrids and are common in urban interface areas. The coy-dog had just killed a deer and was pulling out its guts from the hindquarters when I scared him off. The biggest surprise was not the coyote kill, but that this coyote had killed this deer less than twenty-five feet away from the front door of the neighboring home.

Biologists who are studying coyotes in urban areas say since we can't eradicate them, we will need to learn to live with them. They are teaching us things maybe we don't want to learn yet.

I recently saw an evening news clip from the Chicago area of coyotes running through the streets after dark when the city was quiet. The voiceover of city officials said "No need to be alarmed.

We encourage the coyotes to stick around because they are control-ling the rodent population." With two top predators in an urban environment — men and coyotes — there is a 'nervous harmony' that can be adapted to. Whether we like it or not, coyotes are here to stay. Now isn't it obvious why Coyote was the chosen one — the hero and the fool, the charlatan and the wise One, the creator of the world, irreverent and sacred all at once.

* * * * * *

I was sound asleep when a coyote's singing woke me. My window was cracked and at 2 a.m. the stars were brilliant and glittering in the cool night air. The quarter moon had barely arisen. The stillness of the night was astounding with a hollow reverberation. I could tell he was close, so close I was sure that he was in my front meadows. Over and over he sang his mournful song. A lone coyote calling in that absentee darkness defining a singularity of purpose.

I looked over the edge of my bed: Koda lay unperturbed. No way was he waking up for this song dog. I opened the window wider. His magnetic song awakened a primeval longing for conver-sation deeper than words. It was then I started returning his howls — in poor imitation. Our exchange could have gone on and on, yet I had the distinct feeling I was confusing him. Maybe, I thought, he was one of this years pups, separated from his pack. Here he was calling back and forth with me, when really he was looking for his brothers.

After several minutes of responsive calling, I quieted and with-in just moments I heard them. His family. He heard them too. They were a few miles away on top of the ridge where the pup had been born. As soon as he heard their distant calls, he was gone.

I'd probably even seen this coyote as a pup the spring before in my Wyoming home. That year in May I was taking a short hike looking for spring wildflowers to photograph. We'd had a late and snowy spring, so many of the animals were late in birthing their young. I noticed a narrow steep drainage that appeared to lead to nowhere and was intrigued by the rock formations. I decided to detour and explore. The arroyo was dry, and filled with thick brush. I stayed high, working up the streambed. In short order I was approaching hoo-doo formations along the right side, when I heard some squealing. I looked up in time to see six or seven small furry animals scampering as fast as their little legs could carry them through the shrubbery and into a hole in the weathered rocks. One runt was stuck under some limbs in the drainage, trying to get his rear end to negotiate 'up and over.' Koda was with me; his instinct was to run and explore these little guys, so I called him to my side at a 'stay.'

I was so startled that my first thought had been these were 'kind of big for marmots.' But in an instant I knew they were pups. I got Koda and myself out of there, fearing our smell and intrusion would force the parents to move them. As I was heading down the hillside, I tried to piece together what I just saw? Did I stumble upon a wolf den? Or a coyote den? Thinking about it, I realized that all six pups were the same color. They must have been coyotes.

Comparing these pups to canine puppies, I decided they were around five weeks old. I had read coyotes move their pups out of the den at around seven weeks, so I waited at least a month before heading back to the den site. I wanted to see what it looked like. The few people I told about my sighting warned me not to tell anyone. "Don't say where you saw them or they'll get shot."

What a thought. Cute or not cute, a lot of people just like to kill coyotes for the fun of it. Up here, coyotes don't pose any threat to livestock or chickens. I live next to thousands upon thousands of acres of National Forest, and these coyotes were birthing on Forest Property, far from human habitation. But no matter. People like to kill coyotes, and they're allowed to, designated 'predator status' by Wyoming law.

Sure enough, the pups were gone. The entire site was amazing. The first thing you notice is that this location had been used for years. The bones left in the drainage included everything from old deer's and elk's to birds' and rodents'. I even found a Red Tail Hawk tail feather. I was impressed a coyote could kill a hawk. Above the arroyo was a nice flat area with a small hole where the den was. It looked like someone had taken out a broom and swept

Coyote den. The entire site was amazing.

the area completely clean. The meticulousness of the dirt floor of their den reminded me of a time when I stayed with Tahahumara Indians in their homes while hiking through Copper Canyon. Their houses were simple with dirt floors. Outside was a small corral for the cattle. When you arrived, the host would be sweeping their dirt floor houses as well as a wide perimeter around the outside of the hut. Although it was dirt, they had pride in their homes and kept them clean. These coyote dens were just like that. I didn't have a flashlight, but I used my watch and the sun to reflect light deep inside the den. It was equally clean and went far back. Koda at ninety pounds was way too big to fit into the entrance hole. But the coyote at thirty or forty pounds could easily get inside. Interestingly enough, the tunnel the pups used previously to escape my presence was a secondary entrance. When I examined it, I noticed even another opening. This den had several entrances and exits, which is typical.

A well-worn trail heading straight up the backside of the hill ran from the den. That seemed the likely route of the parents to go on their hunt. Meanwhile, all the brush and fallen limbs in the adjacent dry creek bed provided cover for the pups, as well as a deterrent for predators (and curiosity seekers like myself). This was a premier spot!

The following spring I made my way back to the den site without Koda, in the hopes of snagging some photographs of a new set of pups. My plan was to approach from high up and find a spot to sit. But when I arrived, all was quiet. I watched for a long time, then ventured down to explore. The den site was empty. I could see it hadn't been occupied this year. The old entrance was starting to collect dirt; the hole was smaller through erosion; trails no longer led to and from the den site. I wondered if my presence from the year before had caused the coyotes to abandon it. But then I had another thought.

Several weekends in a row, I'd seen four middle-aged men in hunting fatigues driving around in the truck, two of them hanging off the tailgate, the other two in the front seat. All carried loaded rifles yet hunting season was over. I checked all the spring hunting folders: mountain lions, bears, turkeys. No open season. Coyotes were their obvious target. They were looking for coyotes to shoot for fun, at a time when the females were about to den. They appeared to me like old men playing eleven-year-old-boys' fantasy war games; yet these games were deadly. I remembered the dead coyote Koda had found, half decomposed and eaten, laying on a small rise above a back road where I'd seen their truck cruising. It was April and sweet new grasses were emerging through wet spring snows

And still my question remains: why of all the animals was the

Coyote pup

coyote chosen to represent the hero/trickster? Maybe we North American settlers are beginning to understand the power the coyote held for native peoples for thousands of years. No matter how many coyotes humans have trapped, shot, and poisoned, these canines come back in greater numbers than before. The trickster, shape shifter, and master of the Universe has eluded and outsmarted us again.

One fall I was camping near Jackson at the large, public Gros Vente campground. This campground is for tents, trailers, and RV's. Being late in the season, much of it was empty. A friend who had accompanied me was snug in his small trailer, while I slept alone in my tent — maybe the only person in a tent at the campground. Our dogs were at home because we wanted to explore Teton National Park where no dogs were allowed. Campers all had their 'lights out'; the campground was silent. One coyote began singing and awakened me. He was close by, just in the next empty campsite. I listened for a few moments, then turned over, and went back to sleep. Half asleep, I heard distinct sniffing beside the thin material separating my head from the outside world. In my sleepiness, I thought it was a dog and shooed him away, my hand pounding against the tent. The sniffing continued for a few moments, then stopped. I fell back to sleep. The next morning, I recalled the incident, wondering if it had been a dream. No, it definitely was that song dog, entering into my deeper consciousness through the back door of a dreamtime realm. My friend and I laughed at my own sleepy antics of trying to shoo the dog away. That coyote had fulfilled his emblematic trickster assignment: stumble heartily into the human humdrum world and give them a good chuckle of Awakening.

We need another and a wiser and perhaps a more mystical concept of animals. In a world older and more complete than ours they move finished and complete, gifted with extensions of the senses we have lost or never attained, living by voices we shall never hear. They are not brethren, they are not underlings; they are other nations, caught with ourselves in the net of life and time, fellow prisoners of the splendour and travail of the earth.

Henry Beston 'The Outermost House'

CHAPTER 10

Sacred Land Ethic

Several years ago I visited Uluru in Australia, formerly known as Ayers Rock. My son and I drove to a parking area at dawn. We walked on red earth along a designated path, falling into a deep stillness where all time caved into the Present moment. It had been raining more than usual and the earth was green with new grass, contrasting with soil rich in iron oxide. Occasional signs, powered by small solar units, told the stories of the Dreamtime of Uluru, stories of beings and animals who created many of the features we were seeing in the rocks. There were watering holes where the Anangu women performed ceremonies; rock art and sacred areas where *'No Photography'* signs were posted out of respect to the Anangu. There was no interruption of its numinous beauty with signs about geology, history or explanations of this or that feature. Simply story. Stories of origin and myth. These few signs, the layout of the paths, the attentive simplicity, were all done with a sensitivity to the spiritual force present there. We were entering the church of the Anangu, and to feel the power within this church depended upon the nature of our approach. How everything was designed helped us to approach in the right mood. We began to walk slower, our pace effortlessly synching with the imperceptible breathing of the Land.

The Anangu now manage the Park, closing it for ceremony. Uluru is the women's sacred area; Kata Tjuta nearby is the men's. The entire area sings; the Land draws you into a different posture and conscious awareness. It is an obvious porthole into the Sacred, a container of Spirit. But the power of this place is preserved and amplified through right approach combined with the ceremonies the Anangu perform. Sacred implies and contains the word sacrifice. Humans have long felt that sacrificial gestures in the form of ceremony elicits the Land to respond with good favor and spiritual Presence. The Miwok of California, for instance, performed month long ceremonies during acorn harvest season. They harvested by day and danced every night, singing songs of thanks to the oaks. The other eleven months of the year they honored the trees through various forms of cultivation such as burning, weeding, or using long sticks to whack off dead limbs. The native peoples in my valley sought good hunting favor with the deer through ceremony. So it is with the Anangu of Uluru: like indigenous peoples throughout the world in times past, they are making room for the sacred. The Presence which bleeds through a sacred landscape is akin to a wind blowing through our minds and our bodies, clearing, cleansing, and renewing us.

Another desert, one from my childhood, had a different, irreverent fate. I grew up in Los Angeles, but spent my early childhood Easter weeks with my family in the Palm Springs area. In those days, the late '50s and early '60s, Palm Springs was a tiny town, one main street that bled into the desert within seven or so blocks. Around the edges of the main boulevard lay a vast expanse of arid lands, peppered with a few houses and dirt roads. In nearby Desert

Hot Springs, where healing warm mineral waters push through the San Andreas fault line, there were a few 40s style motels — pink cement buildings surrounded by 'desert rat' style shacks and stores. Date milkshakes were the primary commodity.

It had been years, possibly more than twenty five, since I had last visited this desert. I was shocked at the transformation of my favorite childhood haunt. Saddened more expresses it. Palm Springs and its suburban sister cities are little more than a mini Los Angeles clone, the predominant mindset being this is just empty land to be exploited.

Coachella Valley, where Palm Springs sits, is a unique basin, surrounded on all sides by mountains; it's approximately a forty-five-mile valley landform extending southeast and fifteen miles wide. The spectacular views come from an expanse of Sonoran Desert encased on all sides by mountains, some over 10,000 feet.

Uluru is the women's sacred area

This unique geography creates a deep aquifer of mountain snow runoff. And the aquifer, tapped into, can give life to golf courses and green lawns, and quench the thirst of a steady pilgrimage of sun seekers.

Over the last twenty years, it's become one of the fastest growing areas in the country, now with over half a million full and part-time residents. Drive the wide streets, and you'll find endless miles of shopping center after shopping center, strip malls, housing developments, over 125 golf courses, high end hotels and trophy homes. All press upon what's left of desert, right up to the narrow hillside canyons that rim the valley where coyotes, mountain lions, bighorn sheep and burrowing owls attempt to eke out their own livings.

At the mouth of the valley where cool coastal air mixes with the warm desert air, gale force winds whip the sands into dunes. Thousands of windmills, like giant white sentinels from a futuristic movie, rise from the desert floor to greet the valley's visitors. Plans are in the works to build thousands more on hillocks north and northeast — useless land they say except for its energy potential. In the summer, the area empties out, snowbirds leave, as the thermometer reaches over 115 degrees daily.

There is so much here to lament and offend: habitat loss and fragmentation, water waste (the valley has sunk more than a foot as the aquifer is depleted year by year. Water from the Colorado River is used to slow the subsidence), wanton over-development, noise and light pollution. Yet what is most dispiriting, what never is talked about, is the loss of sensibility and place. What was once the lonesome desert, with views that are found few places on earth, has become just another pedestrian destination, a shrine to over-consumption and recreational distractions. Palm Springs is the representational icon of our dissociation from nature. It is the poster child of what's become our cavernous separation from the land itself.

It is not that I am against building anything at all. But there are ways to plan and build that mix with the landscape; which involve low impact, livable communities and value open land, quiet, and dark skies yet protect habitat and corridors for wildlife and plants. Urban sprawl with same-name big box stores every three miles is not it. There is a path where the lessons of such people and places as the Anangu and their Uluru home can mix with our modern life. We just have to find the threads and follow them. We must become dedicated to following them.

There is an honest experience of spiritual space I believe we all understand deep in our psyches. This knowing comes out of a time when there were fewer of our species on this earth and we banded together for safety. A time when we walked for days without

Thousands of windmills, like giant white sentinels, rise from the desert floor.

seeing another person; when our eye scanned a horizon without limit. Space on our planet is becoming at a premium. Without being told this, we can feel it. Crowd or no crowd, we feel the limit pressing against us. We are aware of this, regardless of how much solitude we enjoy at any moment. And that awareness is troubling — the too-many-rats-in-the-cage syndrome. Our DNA is not fitted for these kinds of crowds. We are adapted for limitlessness, expansiveness, a clarity and freshness of consciousness. All else becomes depressive, constrictive, crazy-making, like a tree caught in a can — its crown gnarled, unable to grow and expand.

Our world today is crowded — even in places where ostensibly it is not. Wires, cell towers, electro-magnetic pollution, air pollution, water pollution, on and on. Earth's overpopulation means we require even larger amounts of sacred spaces, not less, to hold the quiet so necessary for our spiritual peace of mind.

In these last wild places, like the Yellowstone to Yukon Region here in North America, we must do everything we can to protect, preserve, and connect, or else little by little, human erosion will take place and one day we'll wake up and realize what we've lost. Once it's gone for just two generations, it will be completely forgotten. Growing up in a State that was sullied by these strong forces, I'm very sensitive to what can happen in our last refuges of solace.

Preserving wildlife, open spaces, and habitat is the core of Aldo Leopold's term 'land ethic.' He writes:

A thing is right when it tends to preserve the integrity, stability, and beauty of the biotic community. It is wrong when it tends otherwise. The land ethic simply enlarges the boundaries of the community to include soils, waters, plants, and animals, or collectively: the land. [A] land ethic changes the role of Homo sapiens from conqueror of the land-community to plain member and citizen of it. It implies respect for his fellow-members, and also respect for the community as such.

We are members of this biotic community, not users of land for purely economic purposes. Farming or ranching the land is not incongruous to this ethic, but the land ethic holds that these practices are conducted using techniques which benefit the entire biotic community. This is the essential guide for all conservation groups, and for all users of land which means all of us. I believe there is yet another element to the land ethic that must be considered: the ancient relationship to Land as source of vision, spiritual awareness and awakening. The Sacred Land Ethic.

Every great spiritual leader in all traditions — and traditionally any person who had the inclination — went seeking their vision, their connection, a transmission of wisdom or insight through a communion experience in nature. They went alone. Wherever the power was present in their unique geography, there they went. Some to mountains, others to deserts. Some, like the Buddha, found a quiet and large tree to sit under. Others, like the Tibetan Yogi Milarepa, sought a cave and sat there for twenty years. A retreat was necessary, in an isolated sacred spot. The transmission of spiritual awareness in a sacred place seems to have the capacity to transform a person.

Consider this story told to Frank Linderman by Chief Plenty Coups. Vision quests were an egalitarian practice among Indians, not the exclusive right of a few priests. Plenty Coups was a great leader of his people, and the last Chief of the Crows. At the age of nine, in the 1850s, Plenty Coups set off with three other young friends to the Crazy Mountains. All four boys hoped to fulfill their vision quest. Plenty Coups had already completed one unsuccessful such journey (a voice told him *"You did not go to the right mountain"*). Now he was determined more than ever to complete his quest. After fasting for several days and nights, he had a detailed vision. Led by a guide (a Man-Person) under the earth, he walked for many days and nights (in vision time) through a tunnel crowded by buffalo. Then they emerged from the tunnel and sat on a knoll on a hillside.

He (the Man-Person) *shook his red rattle and sang a queer song four times. 'Look!' he pointed.*

Everywhere I looked great herds of buffalo were… pouring out of the hole in the ground to travel on the wide plains. When at last they ceased coming out of the hole in the ground, all were gone, all! There was not one in sight anywhere…

I turned to look at the Man-person beside me. He shook his red rattle again. 'Look!' he pointed.

Out of the hole in the ground came bulls and cows and calves past counting. These, like the others, scattered and spread on the plains. But they stopped in small bands and began to eat the grass. Many lay down, not as a buffalo does but differently, and many were spotted. Hardly any two were alike in color or size. And the bulls bellowed differently too, not deep and far-sounding like bulls of the buffalo but sharper and yet weaker in my ears. Their tails were different, longer, and nearly brushed the ground. They were not buffalo. These were strange animals from another world.

I was frightened and turned to the Man-person, who only shook his red rattle but did not sing. He did not even tell me to look, but I did look and saw all the Spotted-buffalo go back into the hole in the ground, until there was nothing except a few antelope anywhere in sight.

'Do you understand this which I have shown you, Plenty-coups?' he asked me.

'No!' I answered. How could he expect me to understand such a thing when I was not yet ten years old.

Now Plenty Coups and the vision-person went back into the hole and came out again. Now the Man-Person pointed to an old man sitting in the shade, alone, by some trees and square house.

'Look well upon this old man,' said the Man person. 'Do you know him, Plenty-Coups?' he asked me.

'No.'

'This old man is yourself, Plenty-Coups,' he told me.

...And here I am, an old man, sitting under this tree just where that old man sat seventy years ago when this was a different world.

Plenty Coups was an extraordinary man, no doubt about it. But the psychic dimensions he was privy to through his quest are inherent in every man and woman. In today's world where every inch of our globe is not only mapped but visitable on Google Earth, are there any enclaves of potency where 21st century seekers can retreat for our vision quests? How much breathing space does the *Land need* in order to be a vessel of the sacred? If the biotic community is fragmented, does the Land suffer in its ability to act as a potent transmitter? These are the questions we must ask when implementing a Forest Service plan or designing communities. Livable and intentionally created communities and cities that grow local foods, use local power sources as much as possible, create pathways of low impact transportation, and employ local versus big box businesses, help to preserve open space and the natural surrounding lands for recreating and relaxing. These are expanses for hiking, biking, even responsible ATV use. But large tracts of wild lands that can support iconic megafauna and intact ecosystems serve a different purpose, and there the land and animals have different needs. Roads, ATV's, and intensive human use have severe impact on wildlife and their movements.

Everything has it's opposite, and where there is the sacred there is the sacrilegious. This is not new; it is only that in ancient times culture dictated these differences. In today's world, Land is not considered in the sphere of the holy. At Uluru, signs and a cultural education center communicate clearly this is sacred land to the Anangu. It is requested people do not climb the rock. Yet people regularly do. And not only climb, but they have played golf there and even done strip tease. Disrespect and antagonism rings in the tone of people who do this. This disregard is found in obviously powerful places like Devil's Tower, Wyoming, (where climbers insist their rights are impinged upon if they have to respect Native American tradition not to climb their holy site), but it's also evident in the ordinary rhythms of everyday commercialism and commerce: man-made monstrosities like wires, roads, buildings, cell towers, oil fields and even large expanses of wind turbines or solar panels diminish the potency of the Land. This too is Land sacrilege.

Learning how to live lightly for the right reasons and not the 'maximize profit' reasons might be difficult in our day and age, but it's an essential and personal decision for each person. How to leave a natural place in a healthier condition requires being there for a time, understanding its weather and wind cycles, its flora and fauna, and the course the land wants to take over a long period. Healthy and biologically diverse ecosystems have more resilience to face the major climate changes ahead. This means managing our public lands differently by ending ecologically damaging practices such as livestock grazing, and reducing off road use by snowmobiles and all-terrain vehicles.

We all need refugios where we can wander for days without seeing a person or even a trail; a place where the natural forces of the Earth — drought, fire, wind — are allowed to shape the Land, where our eyes can come to rest in a limitless horizon; where the ageless drama of Life is played out by the animals that live there. That drama, of life and death, is the primary spiritual predicament we are seeking to understand when we go out alone. To take time out and contemplate, having the complete bio-community surrounding us on these treks, deepens our pondering and awareness of our paradoxical presence on this earth. We are alive, yet, like every living thing around us, subject to death. We sit between these two forces and spend time in solitude. We take a walk and notice the bones from an elk, killed by a wolf, and preyed upon by raptors, crows, and coyotes. We mourn for a killed deer, but rejoice for the bear mother who fattens her cubs for the long winter ahead. In that rawness we are revealed and deepened in our understanding. Through direct contact with our vulnerability we touch new worlds within ourselves.

Protected awe-inspiring Parks like Muir Woods or Yosemite are still the temples they always and anciently have been. Yet it is impossible to have more than a moment's peace, let alone three quiet days of solitude to ponder the Mystery in these crowded places. In today's world, they are touchstones only. They are glimpses of what calls us on the journey, our potential seen from a vantage point. In yesterday's world, they are where we might have gone when seeking spirit guidance. Preserving grand places like that is important. They help us remember what we need and value. But setting aside, in perpetuity, vast tracts of wild lands is stuff for the soul.

From where I sit, at the edge of one of the last vast intact wildernesses in the temperate world, I have a mountain top view of what is wonderful and how fragile it all is. I see the landscape of animals slowly encroached upon, unknowingly subject to the political and social winds of change. With limited room to roam, so tightly managed they are barely allowed their wildness; their fate in this next century may be unknown. Without them, all we have is an empty, and so much more lonely, landscape.

We all need refuges where we can wander for days without seeing a person.

EPILOGUE

Six winters have come and gone since I uprooted myself from the California coast to live in my Wyoming cabin full-time. I've come to track, and know much better, not just the animals living around me, but the slowness through which the seasons move and blend into each other. Life's rhythms become defined by the movement of the wildlife in harmony with the seasons. All of them, from the squirrel to the grizzly, have their unique patterns coincident with food sources and with one another.

Soon after I settled here, a new and wise friend told me "Leslie, don't become involved in the local politics. It will drive you crazy and you'll forget what drew you here."

Of course, over time, I found it impossible to heed that advice. Land defines the life here and every government decision about its use looms large. And it's easy to be involved. Information meetings are mandated and held in the local towns; comments are tallied; then decisions are finalized. You feel you might be able to make a positive difference because so few people live here. But what becomes evident in this process is that these lands belong to all Americans — they are our public lands. Everyone has a voice yet so few exercise it to make that difference. Millions of people visit Yellowstone Park every year and many more backpack, hunt, or horseback ride into the surrounding forests. If all these people, and more, participated with their voice, vote and pen, priorities for wildlife and land preservation, instead of ATV or oil and gas use, would improve.

But tonight I let all those good fights melt away. I walk out into the night air and the brilliance of the evening sky intrudes upon my feelings. The celestial dome above me is packed with star light. The local wolf pack is howling. They've made a kill nearby and with their bellies full, they announce their pleasure into the blackness. A rustling of hooves beats back and forth in the large meadow in front of the house. I go in and grab a high beam flashlight. As I shine it towards the pasture, a thousand eyes stare back at me. The elk herd has come. Disturbed by my dog and the nearby wolves, they move restlessly as my beam tracks only their eyes, focused on me with curiosity and fear. Something so familiar rustles through my bones. My flashlight becomes a torch, my house the village, and I sit with friends around a fire, ten thousand years ago, with this same sea of eyes staring from the darkness. There is an eeriness to it, and a vulnerability. And a rightness. I feel my humanness and my place in the Universe. I am grateful, once again, to be living here, in one of the last places on earth where all things are intact. It is my home, and without any doubt, I praise the wild excellence.

ACKNOWLEDGEMENTS

I want to thank all who work tirelessly to bring back species from the brink. This includes the unrelenting efforts of volunteers, biologists, advocates and politicians who participated in the reintroduction process of the grey wolf. All those who believe that a full suite is the measure of a healthy ecosystem. This work is ongoing. In this complicated new world, species need our help and most especially our cooperation, in sharing this planet.

A big thank you to my editor Lorna Owen, who encouraged me to continue telling the story. Larry Todd for taking the time to show me important sites; Larry Loendorf for his insights into the archaeological remains in my area; Abbie Nelson and Rebecca Steinberg for letting me tag along; Arthur Middleton; Jack and Jane Braten; the Greater Yellowstone Coalition and especially their Cody office; Ric Heasler for his neighborly advice; Warren Murphy for his comments on the manuscript and accompanying me on many of these hikes; Bonnie Rice of the Sierra Club; Dan and Cindy Hartman; Doug Peacock thank you for taking time from your busy schedule for a close read of the manuscript; Ruffin Prevost of Yellowstonegate.com. And I can't forget my dog Koda. I couldn't have done all this hiking in bear country without his vigilant eyes and especially nose.

NOTES

Chapter 3

1. *"Regional groups were named..."* Richard Adams *The Greater Yellowstone ecosystem, soapstone bowls and the Mountain Shoshone*

2. *"The panzoavits, for example..."* Lawrence L. Loendorf & Nancy Medaris Stone *Mountain Spirit. The Sheep Eater Indians of Yellowstone*

3. *"Here we found a few Snake Indians..."* Osborne Russell Diary of a Trapper pp. *"An eye could scarely be cast..."* Osborne Russell ibid pp.

4. *"the message from the record..."* George C. Frison *Prehistoric Hunters of the High Plains pp.* 142-143

5. *A buffalo herd travels straight..."* Frank B. Linderman, *Pretty Shield* pp. 48-49.

6. *"I know a million [buffalo] is a great..."* Larry Barsness *Heads Hides & Horns* p. 21

7. For bison brucellosis information see Buffalo Field Campaign http://www.buffalofieldcampaign.org

Chapter 4

1. *"...knowledge of ungulate distributions..."* Abigail Nelson master's thesis. University of Wyoming

2. For info on moose in Northwest Wyoming, see Scott Becker's master thesis, University of Wyoming

3. *"Beginning in April 1992..."* and *"The first wave of wolf killing ..."* Renee Askins *Shadow Mountain*

4. *"You have to remember wolves and wolf management has nothing..."* Ed Bangs Interview KQED 2012

5. For an overview on ranching and wolves see Christopher Ketcham *Wolves to the Slaughter* in The American Prospect http://prospect.org/article/wolves-slaughter

6. *"They move with such stealth and perfection..."* Jon Young *Seeing through Native Eyes* tape series.

7. A few organizations that are helping ranchers coexist with wolves through innovative practices are Defenders of Wildlife, People and Carnivores, and Blackfoot Challenge. For example see 'Wolves Among the Sheep' on the Defenders of Wildlife blog.

Chapter 5

1. *"that feeling in your stomach of ..."* Pema Chodron *The Places that Scare You*

2. *"What he found from looking at historical..."* Arthur Middleton's masters thesis. University of Wyoming.

3. For an overview of successful and unsuccessful paradigms in world conservation see Caroline Fraser *Rewilding the World.*

Chapter 7

1. There are many organizations using Karelian Bear Dogs. Wind River Bear Institute of Montana works in Canadian Parks as well as the U.S.

    http://www.beardogs.org

2. *"When someone [in a native culture] had..."* David Rockwell *Giving Voice to Bear.*

3. *"I recognized them easily..."* William H. Wright *The Grizzly Bear*

4. *"thin..., moderate to numerous numbers of tapeworms..."* p. 10 Investigation Team Report—Bear Attacks in the Soda Butte Campground on July 28, 2010

5. See The Yellowstone to Yukon Conservation Initiative http://y2y.net

Chapter 8

1. Early stories of Dead Indian Hill from *Pony Trails of Wyoming* by John K. Rollinson

2. Allie Ritterbrown's unpublished manuscript

3. *"In bad weather…"* Dr. Dewitt Dominick *Doctor Dewey*

4. http://foresthistory.org/ASPNET/Publications/region/2/shoshone/sec2.htm see Frank Hammitt's grave

Chapter 9

1. Barry Lopez *Giving Birth to Thunder Sleeping with his Daughter* p. xiv

2. http://www4.hmc.edu:8001/humanities/indian/ca/ch08.htm; Tad Beckman, Harvey Mudd College, Claremont, CA 91711]

3. Dr. Robert Crabtree quotes from a published letter June 21, 2012 to Wildlife Services, requested by Brooks Fahy, Executive Director of Predator Defense http://www.thewildlifenews.com/wp-content/uploads/2012/07/Crabtrees-Letter-on-Coyotes.pdf

4. Paul Radin *The Trickster* 1956 (xxiii).

Chapter 10

1. *"We need another…"* Beston *The Outermost House*

2. *"A thing is right…"* Aldo Leopold *A Sand County Almanac* p. 204

3. *"I turned to look…"* Frank Linderman *Plenty Coups Chief of the Crows* pp. 35-36.

FOR ADDITIONAL READING

A Sand County Almanac by Aldo Leopold. Oxford University Press 1949.

Advanced Bird Language. Reading the Concentric Rings of Nature and Seeing Through Native Eyes, by Jon Young., Eight Audio CD set available at www.WildernessAwareness.org.,

Animal Skulls A guide to North American Species, by Mark Elbroch.,

Behavior of North American Mammals, by Mark Elbroch and Kurt Rinehart. Houghton Mifflin Harcourt. 2011.,

Botany in a Day. Their Patterns Method of Plant Identification., by Thomas J. Elpel., Hops Press 2008.,

Buffalo for the Broken Heart. Restoring life to a Black Hills Ranch, by Dan O'Brien., Random House. 2002

Doctor Dewey: Stories from the Life and Career of Dr. Dewitt Dominick of Cody Wyoming by Dr. Dewitt Dominick and Mary Dominick Chivers. Wordsworth. 2004.

Giving Birth to Thunder. Sleeping with his Daughter. Coyote Builds North America by Barry Lopez. Avon 1977

Giving Voice to Bear: North American Indian Myths, Rituals, and Images of the Bear by David Rockwell 2003

Heads, Hides & Horns. The Compleat Buffalo Book, by Larry Barsness., TCU Press 1985.,

Hiking with Grizzlies. Lessons Learned, by Tim Rubbert, Riverbend Publishing

Kill the Cowboy A Battle of Mythology in the New West by Sharman Russell. Bison Books 2001

Mammal Tracks & Sign. A Guide to North American Species, by Mark Elbroch. Stackpole Books 2003.,

Plenty-Coups. Chief of the Crow, by Frank B. Linderman., Bison Books reprint 2002, originally published in 1930.,

Pony Trails of Wyoming by John K. Rollinson. The Caxton Printers, Ltd. 1941

Prehistoric Hunters of the High Plains, by George C. Frison., Academic Press 1991.,

Pretty-Shield Medicine Woman of the Crows by Frank B. Linderman. University of Nebraska Press. 2003

Restoring a Presence. American Indians and Yellowstone National Park, by Peter Nabokov and Lawrence Loendorf., University of Oklahoma Press. 2004.,

Ancient Visions. Petroglyphs and Pictographs of the Wind River and Bighorn Country, Wyoming and Montana, by Julie E. Francis and Lawrence L. Loendorf. University of Utah Press. 2002.,

Mountain Spirit. The Sheep Eater Indians of Yellowstone, by Lawrence L. Loendorf & Nancy Medaris Stone., University of Utah Press 2006.,

Rewilding the World. Dispatches from the Conservation Revolution, by Caroline Fraser., Picador Press 2009.

Sacred Cows at the Public Trough, by Nancy Ferguson., Maverick Publishing 1983.,

Seeing through Native Eyes by Jon Young. Owling Media 1996

Seven Half-Miles from Home. Notes of a Wind River Naturalist by Mary Back. Johnson Books 1985.

Shadow Mountain. A Memoir of Wolves, a Woman and the Wild, by Renee Askins. Anchor Books. 2002.

Stories of the Eastern Shoshone told by John Trehero to Ake Hultkrantz Mortimore Publishing 2009

The Abstract Wild, by Jack Turner. University of Arizona 1996.

The Grizzly Bear by William H. Wright. University of Nebraska Press. 1977. Reprinted from the original 1908.

The Grizzly Years: In Search of the American Wilderness by Doug Peacock. Henry Holt & Co. 1990.

The Influence of Large Carnivore recovery and Summer Conditions on the Migratory Elk of Wyoming's Absaroka Mountains by Arthur Middleton 2012. Ph.D. Dissertation, University of Wyoming.

The Light in High Places, by Joe Hutto. Skyhorse Publishing 2009.,

The Man Made of Words by N. Scott Momaday. St. Martins's Press 1997

The Outermost House. A year of life on the great beach of Cape Cod by Henry Beston. Henry Holt and Company 1949.

The Places That Scare You by Pema Chodron. Shambhala 2002

The Practice of the Wild by Gary Snyder. North Point Press 1990.

The Solace of Open Spaces by Gretel Ehrlich. Penguin Books 1985

The Trickster. A Study in American Indian Mythology by Paul Radin. Routledge & Kegan Paul 1956.

The Wild Within. Adventures in Nature and Animal Teachings by Paul Rezendes Penguin Putnam Inc. 1998.

Trampling the Public Trust by Debra L. Donahue. Boston College Environmental Affairs Law Review Volume 37, Issue 2, Article 2. January 2010.

Track of the Grizzly by Franck C. Craighead, Jr. Sierra Club Books 1979.

Winter Garden by Pablo Neruda translated by William O'Daly. 1986 Copper Canyon Press.

Wolfer. A Memoir, by Carter Niemeyer., Bottlefly Press 2010.,

Yellowstone Bears in the Wild, by James C. Halfpenny. Riverbend Publishing. 2007

Yellowstone Rising by Lynne Bama. Pronghorn Press

Leslie Patten is a landscape designer with a background in tracking and naturalist studies. She is the author of *Biocircuits: Amazing New Tools for Energy Health* as well as several eBooks on Gardening.

Her design website is *www.ecoscapes.net*.

Her blog is *www.thehumanfootprint.wordpress.com*

CPSIA information can be obtained
at www.ICGtesting.com
Printed in the USA
FSOW04n0821070316
17562FS